Best Buys
and Bargains in Paris

Best Buys and Bargains in Paris

(Yes, they do exist!)

by
Jeanne Feldman,
an American in Paris

Writers Club Press
San Jose New York Lincoln Shanghai

Best Buys and Bargains in Paris
(Yes, they do exist!)

Writers Club Press
an imprint of iUniverse.com, Inc.

For information address:
iUniverse.com, Inc.
620 North 48th Street, Suite 201
Lincoln, NE 68504-3467
www.iuniverse.com

Cover photographs by Jeanne Feldman

ISBN: 0-595-12522-0

Printed in the United States of America

I dedicate this guide first of all to my parents,
the King and Queen of discount.

CONTENTS

PREFACE

Why did I write this guide? I suppose that in the end, genes won out. Let's just say, that in my family, as in Woody Allen's *Radio Days*, the worst sin in the family was to buy retail. So, I am merely continuing the family tradition.

I'm American, but I've lived in Paris since 1991. Shopping here is a challenge, believe me since, no doubt about it, Paris is a very expensive city. Fortunately, if you know where to look, discounts, bargains and best buys are available. My idea of "best buy" is to find the best quality for the lowest price. So, not every item in the guide is low in price, but it certainly has the best price considering its value.

Like you, I want quality, but I don't like to waste my time. So, I did all the work for you! I visited each store personally, but only kept the good ones. I don't claim to have listed every great store in Paris, but, what I have done is to list the great stores I like. You may very well find a terrific store near you that is not listed in this guide. That's great, and I certainly would appreciate getting your comments by email or "snail mail" for corrections and additions to the next guide. But at least you know that each store has passed the Feldman quality test!

Although I have visited each store personally, I have not visited all the branch stores. So if I list them because of a convenient location, I can't totally vouch for the same conditions as in the "mother" store.

Many of the shop owners don't even know they are in this guide. But, I'm sure they'd be pleased if you show them their listing.

ACKNOWLEDGEMENTS

I would like to thank all my friends and family who supported me while I researched and wrote this guide. I also want to thank them for helping me with ideas, and even with editing. Last, but not least, I want to thank Dallas and Nan Patten, the inspirations for this guide—thanks Dallas and Nan!

Introduction

How the Guide Is Organized

Each section is either arranged geographically, by *arrondissement* (section), and then by Métro stop, or alphabetically when the chapter is small.

Within each section, listings are preceded by "key words" in italics which summarize the entry. So, when you look through the list, you can easily scan these key words, rather than having to read all the text. This should be especially helpful if you are looking for something specific.

Why Shopping Etiquette?

When you live in or visit France, basically you're lulled into a false sense of security. After all, you say, it's a western country with a similar culture to your own. Wrong! What they don't tell you is that going to France is like going to Asia in terms of cultural differences, only in Asia you have the advantage of knowing this in advance. People do things and see things in a way you could never imagine! The unwritten rules are different. Expectations are different. How people relate to one another is different. So, you need to know some basic rules of "shopping etiquette" in order to relate to French sales people or, believe me, misunderstandings will occur.

The French Are not Rude, They're Just Serious

Of course, from time to time you'll find someone who is rude, just like anywhere else, but if you follow my advice, you'll be surprised how polite

French people really are. Not humorous, smiley, or joking, but definitely polite. This is what to do: pretend you were born in Atlanta, Georgia before the Civil War and Scarlett O'Hara is your best friend. That is, be very, very polite and a bit formal. Try to speak in French, even if your French isn't great. So, instead of blurting out, "Can you tell me where're the women's clothes are?," in one breath, say instead, "Bonjour." (wait for a response), "Pourriez-vous me dire où se trouve les vêtements femme?" (Hello. Could you please tell me where the women's clothes are?). Very important—the first words out of your mouth addressing any merchant or sales person (French) must be "bonjour" (hello), or "excusez-moi" (excuse me) and then wait for the response. It also helps if you have a problem ("j'ai un problème"). I'm not kidding.

Store Etiquette

In France, when you enter a small store or a department store, the first thing you have to do is scan the premises for the sales person, locate them and then say, "bonjour" (hello) with confidence. I know this seems like a simple thing, but, believe me, it makes all the difference in the world. If you do this, you will be well treated. If you do not, you won't. It's that simple. Then, when you leave, say "au revoir" (goodbye). Say goodbye, even if you haven't bought a thing. This demonstrates that you are well mannered and are, therefore, a worthy customer. In addition, many merchants will test you by offering the worst of the lot. Don't accept it. It is perfectly acceptable to refuse (politely, of course) and demand exactly and specifically what you want. The pickier you are, the more the merchant or sales person will respect you. One small warning: none of the above may apply in a large department store where the sales staff can act as if customers are a minor inconvenience interrupting their day. But you can try anyway. You never know.

They're not in It for the Money

Yes, that's right. French merchants can be downright anti-commercial. Many of the small shop keepers are operating a family-run business and/or they are doing something they are interested in and are experts at. Money is definitely not at the top of their list. So, do not expect them to bend over backwards to serve you. They will do this if you have a problem or you captivate their interest, but not just for the money. It also makes a big difference if they know you or not. France basically has a Latin culture which is based on personal relationships. So, if the merchant knows you, he or she will treat you very well. If not, it depends on how polite and *bien élevé* (well mannered) you are.

Standing in Line (or not as the Case May Be)

French people are not into standing in line; certainly, not a straight one. (One exception to this is in the bakery.) The hidden message seems to be, time is not important. So, if you get there first, that does not guarantee you're going to be served first. After all, life isn't always fair, is it? What really counts is geography, i.e. who is nearest rather than who is first. One way you can counter this is to pay strict attention to who is at the counter before you, and when it's your turn, you say firmly, "C'est à moi" (it's my turn). This usually works.

Your Way Is Blocked and They Don't Move Out of the Way

When people block your way, they won't move until you give them a signal. That signal is to say, "pardon," and then slip gently but firmly through. They will move (although sometimes belatedly).

A Little Shopping Vocabulary

FRENCH	ENGLISH
braderie	discount or rummage sale
brocante	secondhand that is not antique
C'est à moi	It's my turn (!)
dame or femme	woman
démarque	markdown
enfant	child
flacon	perfume bottle
homme	man
J'aimerais jeter un coup d'oeil.	I'd like to take a look.
Je regarde, merci.	I'm just looking, thanks.
poussez	push
soldes	sales
sonnez	ring (the bell or buzzer)
tel quel	as is
tirez	pull
vendu	sold
vêtements	clothes/clothing

The Floors Are Different

In France, the 1st floor U.S. is the ground floor (*rez-de-chaussée*) which means exactly what it says, i.e. level with the ground, and the 2nd floor U.S. is the 1st floor, etc.

Getting the Most Out of Your Money

Shopping Is Different Here

So, you've just run out of shampoo and don't want to spend an arm and a leg to replace it before you can get back to your regular beauty supply store at home? Where to go? I advise going to the nearest Monoprix (the equivalent of a variety store and supermarket combined in one store). Look in the shampoo section (*shampooing*) and buy L'Oréal Elsève Shampooing Soin Fortifiance and Après-Shampooing in golden-yellow bottles. This is a new line from L'Oréal easily and cheaply available in France and it is quite good. If that is not in stock, buy Jacques Dessange which is not quite as good, but works fine and is inexpensive. I especially like the yellow label for damaged hair. Basic hair vocabulary: *shampooing* (you can guess what this is), *après-shampooing* which is cream rinse and *masque* which is conditioner. *Soin* as it's used here means beauty treatment. You can now also find Pantene Pro-V hair products in France which are a bit more expensive but are great too.

The closest equivalent to a drug store is the *Parapharmacie* which has the best selection of dental products (tooth brushes, pastes, floss, etc.). The prices are a bit high compared with Britain and the US, but at least you have the selection. You can also find beauty products, soaps, etc.

Store Cards

Many stores have a *carte de fidelité* or a store discount card which entitles you to a refund or discount after making a certain number of purchases. So, if you think you will be shopping regularly in one particular store, ask if they have this card. (You've got to ask as the store will rarely volunteer this information.)

Value Added Tax Refund

How the value added tax (VAT) refund works: All prices listed in the stores already include a tax of 19.6%, recently reduced from 20.6%. That means if the goods are worth 1000 francs, you have to pay 196 francs in tax. So, the price listed in the store is 1196 francs. If you are a non-European citizen, you can generally get a refund on this tax if you spend at least 1200 francs per store in one day. If you pay by credit card, they can create a charge credit for the amount of the refund before you leave the store. Then you have to fill out special forms in the store (for which you'll need your passport number) which you will show to a special customs window before you check your bags or go through regular customs at your final destination in Europe. They will validate the forms, then you or they will send them back to the store, at which time they will credit your account or send you a refund check in French francs (good luck). In conclusion, it's a lot easier if you pay by credit card! The amount you get back is about 16% of the total price except in the department stores where you will be refunded about 13%.

Price Ranges

Since exchange rates fluctuate, I have not chosen to list specific prices. Instead, I give a price range of low, medium or high. Generally speaking, low means up to 250 FF; medium means 250 to 500 FF, and high is over 500 FF. However, as in real life, it's all relative! So, if an item worth 3000 FF is selling for 1500 FF, the price is not low objectively, but it's low for the value. So, I do my best to make this distinction when giving the price range of the store.

Changing Money

The very best way to change money is to withdraw cash from an automatic teller machine at a bank or post office. You get the best rate, no commission is charged and the amount is deducted from your account on your next bank statement at home. If you choose instructions in English, don't worry—the money will be French! If you've got two cards, bring both in case one gets lost, demagnetized or "swallowed" by an angry French ATM! In addition, French credit cards have PIN's of 4 digits maximum (no letters), so your card should have the same number of digits. If you've got letters, memorize them as numbers. One problem is that if you have a Plus or Cirrus card, many Paris banks are not yet linked up with the international computers, so you may have to try several before finding the right one. One bank that I have had success with is Bred Banque Populaire. Warning: if you get an error signal, stop immediately and try another bank. After three try's, the ATM will swallow your card and the bank may even destroy it! (Three strikes and you're out—I speak from personal experience here.)

The second best way to change money is to find a money-change. Sometimes I go to the rue de Vivienne, which runs along the Bourse (stock exchange), Métro Bourse. The whole street is wall to wall money changes, no commission and they all have the same rate which is pretty good. They are open Monday to Friday during business hours. If it's the weekend and/or the rue de Vivienne is not convenient, here are some other changes with excellent rates.

BENLUX PARIS DUTY FREE
174 rue de Rivoli, 1st arrondissement
Métro Palais Royal, Change open every day 10 to 6 (opens Sunday 11),
Tel: 01 42 96 89 44

SOCIETE FRANCAISE DE CHANGE
21 rue Chanoinesse, 4th arrondissement
Métro Cité, Open every day 9:30 to 7, Tel: 01 43 26 01 84

CHANGE DU CLARIDGE
74 avenue des Champs Elysées (at the back of the mall), 8th arrondissement
Métro Franklin D. Roosevelt, Open Monday to Saturday 10 to 6:45

BANQUE LIBANAISE POUR LE COMMERCE
7 rue Auber, 9th arrondissement

Métro Opéra/RER Auber, Open Monday to Friday 9 to 5, Tel: 01 47 42 33 89

BUREAU DE CHANGE
94 boulevard Rochechouart, 18th arrondissement
Métro Anvers or Pigalle, Open every day 8:30 to 9:30, Tel: 01 42 55 79 27

Getting Around Paris

How Paris Is Organized Geographically

Paris is organized by districts called *arrondissement*s. To those of us who live here, this is essential information. The *arrondissement* is the number (1 to 20) following the address. Basically, it starts in the center of Paris around Notre Dame with the first *arrondissement* (although the cathedral itself is officially in the 4th *arrondissement* directly adjacent) and moves like a snail through Paris in a clockwise direction.

Here is a short list of some of the major monuments and/or places of interest in each arrondissement:

First arrondissement:	the Louvre and the Jardin des Tuilleries
Second arrondissement:	the Bourse (stock market) and the Bibliothèque Nationale de France
Third arrondissement:	Musée Carnavalet
Fourth arrondissement:	the Pompidou Center, Notre Dame and Place des Vosges
Fifth arrondissement:	the Latin Quarter and Jardin des Plantes

Sixth arrondissement: the Sorbonne, Eglise Saint-Germain-des-Prés and the Luxembourg Gardens

Seventh arrondissement: Invalides and the Eiffel Tower

Eighth arrondissement: avenue des Champs Elysées and the Arc de Triomphe

Ninth arrondissement: Opéra Garnier and the department stores Printemps and Galeries Lafayette

Tenth arrondissement: Gare du Nord, Gare de l'Est and the Canal Saint-Martin

Eleventh and twelfth arrondissements: Opéra Bastille and Parc de Bercy

Thirteenth arrondissement: Paris Chinatown and the Bibliothèque Nationale de Tolbiac

Fourteenth arrondissement: Observatoire de Paris, the Catacombs and Parc Montsouris

Fifteenth arrondissement: Parc George Brassens and Parc André Citroën

Sixteenth arrondissement: Trocadéro and Maison de Radio France

Seventeenth arrondissement: Palais des Congrès

Eighteenth arrondissement: Sacré-Coeur and Montmartre

Nineteenth arrondissement: Parc des Buttes Chaumont, Cité des Sciences et de l'Industrie and La Villette

Twentieth arrondissement: Cimetière du Père Lachaise

Be Careful About the Street Names and Numbers

Sometimes different streets have almost the same name. For example, you've got rue Montmartre, boulevard Montmartre and rue de Faubourg Montmartre which are three separate streets all in the same area. You may also find several entrances to the same building with the same street number. So, look at all the entrances in the building to find the store you're looking for. Also, the odd numbers of the street are often not at all related to the even numbers just opposite. This means that if you are looking for number 34, don't expect it to be opposite number 35 (it may be, but probably not!).

Metro Maps

To find the stores, you can use the detailed street maps posted in each Métro station which include a diagram of the stairs leading up from each exit. These maps are great to use to get your bearings. You can usually find them on the wall near the main exit of the station, except in some cases where there are several main exits and then you can find them posted on the platform.

Map Books

If you really want to find some of the more obscure (but definitely worth going to) stores listed in this guide, I suggest you invest in a map book of Paris organized by arrondissement. You can find them in most bookstores or newspaper kiosks in Paris.

The Telephone

When you call a number in Paris, all numbers are preceded by 01. However, if you call from outside France, you must dial the country code 33, then the Paris code **which is 1 without the 0**, and then the number. If you make calls from a phone booth in France, you'll need a Télécarte which you can buy at the Post Office, any *tabac* or at Monoprix (the French variety store). The price is the same everywhere and you pay by the unit. Some bars and cafés still have phones that take change.

BOOKSTORES: ENGLISH LANGUAGE

NEW & USED PAPERBACKS
THE ABBEY BOOKSHOP/LA LIBRAIRIE CANADIENNE
29 rue de la Parcheminerie, 5th arrondissement
Métro St Michel/RER St Michel
Open Monday to Saturday 10 to 7
Tel: 01 46 33 16 24/Fax: 01 46 33 03 33/email address:

It's hard to miss the Canadian flag flying over the door! They've got a pretty good selection of new and used paperback books. If you have books to sell back, they offer 1/3 the value of the book in trade for another book or 1/4 the value in cash. You can order books ahead of time to be mailed to your hotel. Just send them an order by fax including your credit card number and signature and allow 4 to 5 days for delivery. Postage and handling costs 25 F for the first book and 15 F for each additional book.

FRENCH TEXT BOOKS
ATTICA
64 rue de la Folie Méricourt, 11th arrondissement
Métro Oberkampf
Web Site: http://www.attica-langues.com
Open Tuesday to Saturday 10 to 7, Monday 2 to 7
Tel: 01 49 29 27 27

Although most of this large warehouse of a store is filled with textbooks to learn English, Attica also has one of the best selections of French textbooks to learn French. In the back of the store is the *Polyglotte* room where all the other languages except English are kept. You'll find grammar books, French courses, self-taught courses, business dictionaries, exercise books, cassettes and more.

AUSTRALIAN SUBJECT MATTER
AUSTRALIAN BOOKSHOP
33 quai des Grands Augustins, 6th arrondissement
Métro St Michel/RER St Michel
Open Tuesday to Sunday 11 to 7
Tel: 01 43 29 08 65

All the books in this store contain Australian subject matter (of course!) including books on the Aborigines, aboriginal art and children's books. They also have postcards and posters.

NEW HARD COVERS & PAPERBACKS
BRENTANO'S
37 avenue de l'Opéra, 2nd arrondissement
Métro Opéra
Open Monday to Saturday 10 to 7:30
Tel: 01 42 61 52 50

This is one of two main English language bookstores in Paris. The store winds around the back and has an excellent selection of new hardback and paperback books in many categories. No used books here, but you will often find promotional books at excellent prices which include end of series, and publishers' close-outs. In addition, a *Client Privilégié* card is available entitling you to a 5% discount. Brentano's also has regular poetry readings and book signings. You can find out the schedule in two ex-pat publications: *FUSAC* (France USA Contacts) and *The Paris Free Voice*. Both can be found in the store. They are also available in American/British restaurants, Irish pubs and at The American Church (65 quai d'Orsay, 7th, Métro Invalides or Alma-Marceau, Tel: 01 40 62 05 00).

SERIOUS ATMOSPHERE
GALIGNANI BOOKSELLER
224 rue de Rivoli, 1st arrondissement
Métro Tuileries
Open Monday to Saturday 10 to 7
Tel: 01 42 60 76 07

As it states on the outside of the shop, Galignani is an "English, American and French bookshop with an international fine arts department." The atmosphere is very hushed—this is a serious bookstore! There are some magazines and a good selection of new paperback books.

METAPHYSICAL
GOLDEN BOOKS
3 rue de Larochelle, 14th arrondissement
Métro Edgar Quinet or Gaîté
Open Tuesday to Saturday 1 to 7
Tel: 01 43 22 38 56

This is Paris' one and only English esoteric bookstore. In one small room you will find, "Eastern Development, New Sciences, Astrology and Metaphysics, Natural Medicine." The owner speaks English and is very helpful.

GRAPHICS & DESIGN
LIBRAIRIE DOBKINE
53 bis Quai des Grands Augustins, 6th arrondissement

Métro St Michel/RER St Michel
Open Monday to Saturday 1 to 8
Tel: 01 43 26 63 11

In this hole in the wall store you will find an excellent collection of art, graphics, design and fashion books. They also have some auction catalogs and music scores.

NEW PAPERBACKS
NOUVEAU QUARTIER LATIN
78 boulevard St Michel, 6th arrondissement
RER Luxembourg
Open Monday to Saturday 10 to 7
Tel: 01 43 26 42 70

The headings are in French, but the books are in English in this bookstore. They specialize in paperbacks. No used books.

USED BOOKS
SAN FRANCISCO BOOK CO.
17 rue Monsieur le Prince, 6th arrondissement
Métro Odéon
Open Monday to Saturday 11:15 to 9, Sunday 2 to 9
Tel: 01 43 29 15 70

You will find mostly used books in this small, densely packed store, and some of the prices are very low indeed. They buy back books at about 5 F per book if the book is in good condition and they think they can sell it. Service is friendly (one of the owners is American).

NEW & USED BOOKS
SHAKESPEARE AND COMPANY

37 rue de la Bûcherie, 5th arrondissement
Métro St Michel/RER St Michel
Open every day noon to midnight
Tel: 01 43 26 96 50

If you want atmosphere, this is it. The original Shakespeare and Company was a major gathering place for English and American writers in France. It was owned by Sylvia Beach who first published James Joyce's *Ulysses* after an obscenity trial in 1921 prevented its publication in Britain or the U.S. In that same year she moved Shakespeare from the Rue de l'Odéon to its present location, and the current owner George Whitman, continues to support writers and poets, as is proven by the sofa beds on the upper floor! (As a matter of fact, he is the great grandson of Walt Whitman.) Amidst the jumble, you can find both new and used books. If you have books to sell, try to come to the store between noon and 4. There are also poetry and other readings.

USED PAPERBACKS
TEA AND TATTERED PAGES
24 rue Mayet, 6th arrondissement
Métro Duroc
Open every day 11 to 7
Tel: 01 40 65 94 35

You won't find the most recent best sellers, but the store is really packed with books and you can always find something. They buy back paperback books (if they think they can resell them) at 2 to 5 F per book. If they do, you get a 10% discount off the price of books you buy that day. In addition, they have a store card (*carte de fidelité*) where they add up your purchases. When you get to 250 F, you get an additional 25 F off your next purchase. The decision to buy or not is made by the owner who is there 3 to 4 times a week, usually not during the weekends. So, if she isn't there when you arrive, you have to leave the books until she has a chance to evaluate them. There is also a tea room where they serve snacks and desserts.

INTELLECTUAL
VILLAGE VOICE BOOKSHOP

6 rue Princesse, 6th arrondissement
Métro Mabillon
Open Monday 2 to 8, Tuesday to Saturday 10 to 8
Tel: 01 46 33 36 47

The name says it all. You feel as if you're in a sophisticated New York City bookstore—very high level and intellectual. The owner, Odile Hillier, stocks both hardbacks and paperbacks, but no used books, although she has some new books at a reduced price.

NEW HARDBACKS & PAPERBACKS
WH SMITH

248 rue de Rivoli, 1st arrondissement
Métro Concorde
Open Monday to Saturday 9:30 to 7, Sunday 1 to 6
Tel: 01 44 77 88 99

This is the second major English language bookstore in Paris for new books, mostly paperbacks. They also sell greeting cards plus an excellent selection of British and American newspapers and magazines. Be sure to ask for a 5% reduction card which you can sign up for right in the store. The schedule for poetry readings and book signings can be found in FUSAC and The Paris Free Voice (see Brentano's listing).

Chocolate, Bread & Pastries

Introduction

One of the great if not the greatest thing about Paris is the food. Besides the gourmet supermarkets listed in this guide, there are numerous specialty stores, far too many to list. Following are a few of my favorite shops in Paris for chocolate, bread and pastries.

BEST BUY TIP: In the Monoprix supermarket chain they sell their own brand of chocolate called *Monoprix Gourmet*. It's yummy, good quality and not expensive at all. I also like the brand *Poulain* which is sold in many supermarkets. Look for the number "1848" on the front of packaging.

Chocolate

First Arrondissement

OLD FASHIONED CHOCOLATE
CHARLES CHOCOLATIER
15 rue Montorgueil, 1st arrondissement
Métro/RER Les Halles
Open Monday 2 to 7:45, Tuesday to Saturday 10 to 7:45
Tel: 01 45 08 57 77

They make old-fashioned chocolate in this shop which means no milk, butter or cream. Just chocolate…concentrated chocolate. A must for "chocoholics."

Second Arrondissement

TOP QUALITY
TERROIRS
21 passage Choiseul, 2nd arrondissement
Métro Quatre Septembre
Open Monday to Saturday 11 to 7, Sunday 2 to 7
Tel: 01 42 96 56 56

The chocolates here are of the highest quality, on a par with the best, for a medium price. In other words, they're fantastic! They also sell a candy called *Les Conquises de Conques*, made of oranges, hazelnuts, and carob among other ingredients. They taste even better than they sound. The rest of the food items in the store, such as mustard, oil, vinegar, etc., are regional specialties from the south west of France.

Fourth Arrondissement

CANDY AND BOXED CHOCOLATE
GIRARD
4 rue des Archives, 4th arrondissement
Métro Hôtel de Ville
Open Tuesday to Saturday 9:30 to 6:30
Tel: 01 42 72 39 62

Located on a busy street, opposite the department store BHV, the old-fashioned store feels as if you've entered another time and place. They have a beautiful assortment of candy and chocolate in boxes and sacks. Take your time and sample some of the *dragées*, (candy coated almonds) made in their own factory. They also have *marrons glacés* (glazed chestnuts). The prices are amazingly reasonable.

Sixth Arrondissement

FRESH CHOCOLATE FROM THE SOUTH OF FRANCE
PUYRICARD
106 rue du Cherche Midi, 6th arrondissement
Métro Duroc or Vaneau
Open Tuesday to Thursday 10 to 7, Friday & Saturday 10 to 8
Tel: 01 42 84 20 25

The chocolate comes direct from the South of France to this sales outlet. Considering the high quality and that they use all natural ingredients, the price is reasonable.

Other location:
27 avenue Rapp, 7th arrondissement, Métro Pont de l'Alma, Tel: 01 47 05 59 47

Seventh Arrondissement

NOT DISCOUNT BUT GO ANYWAY
DEBAUVE ET GALLAIS
30 rue des Saints Pères, 7th arrondissement
Métro St Germain
Open Monday to Saturday 9 to 7
Tel: 01 40 39 05 50

You feel as if you've entered a jewelry store rather than a chocolate shop here. This is among the best chocolate in Paris, founded in 1800 by an apothecary and former supplier of chocolate to His Majesty King Louis XVI. The prices are high, but it's very high quality.

Other locations:

33 rue Vivienne, 2nd arrondissement, Métro Bourse

107 rue Jouffroy d'Abbans, 17th arrondissement, Métro Etoile or Monceau

Eighth Arrondissement

THE ULTIMATE CHOCOLATE EXPERIENCE
LA MAISON DU CHOCOLAT
225 Faubourg St Honoré, 8th arrondissement
Métro Ternes
Open Monday to Saturday 9:30 to 7:30
Tel: 01 42 27 39 44

Many people say this is the best chocolate in Paris, if not the world!. We won't talk about price here!.

Other locations:

19 rue de Sèvres, 6th arrondissement, Métro Sèvres-Babylone, Tel: 01 45 44 20 40

52 rue François Iᵉʳ, 8th arrondissement, Métro Franklin D. Roosevelt, Tel: 01 47 23 38 25

8 boulevard de la Madeleine, 9th arrondissement, Métro Madeleine, Tel: 01 47 42 86 52

89 avenue Raymond Poincaré, 16th arrondissement, Métro Victor Hugo, Tel: 01 40 67 77 83

Ninth Arrondissement

CHOCOLATE, CANDY, JAM AND HONEY

A LA MERE DE FAMILLE
35 rue du Faubourg Montmartre, 9th arrondissement
Métro Grands Boulevards
Open Tuesday to Friday 8:30 to 1:30 and 3 to 7, Saturday 8:30 to 12:45 and 3 to 7

You will find a large variety of candy and chocolate in this store, founded in 1761 and still in the same location. The neighborhood is not very charming, but the store is. They also sell jams and preserves, tea, honey, and dried fruit. The chocolate is delicious and a bit less expensive than in the more luxurious neighborhoods.

Fifteenth Arrondissement

WHOLESALE CANDIES
CONFISERIE EN GROS
72 boulevard de Grenelle, 15th arrondissement
Métro Dupleix
Open Tuesday to Saturday 9:15 to 7, Monday 2 to 7
Tel: 01 45 79 79 42

Join the line of French grannies buying boxes of chocolates and candy plus glazed chestnuts at cut-rate prices. The selection here is very good.

Eighteenth Arrondissement

HAND-MADE CHOCOLATE
CAPRICES
41 rue des Abbesses, 18th arrondissement
Métro Abbesses
Open Tuesday to Sunday 9:30 to 8
Tel: 01 46 20 29

Caprices is a good example of a small neighborhood chocolate store. They have a good selection of hand-made chocolates for reasonable prices.

BEST BUY TIP: There are a lot of small stores like Caprices all over Paris where they make their own chocolate, and it's delicious. Once your leave the tourist areas, you'll find them.

BREAD

NOTE: The latest trend in bread is old-fashioned (*pain à l'ancienne*) which uses a blend of flours and is made by hand. You can now find wonderful naturally made bread at most of the outdoor markets. There are also more and more local bakeries (*boulangeries*) that excel in old style bread in contrast to the industrially produced bread found in the supermarkets. The industrial bread is cheaper, but it cannot compare with the handmade. (I hate to admit it, but sometimes you get what you pay for.)

It can be a little confusing in the bakery because there are a lot of different breads and each bakery is different. In general, the standard bread is the baguette, the famous long and thin bread with a golden crust. You can buy a *demie baguette* or half a baguette if you want.

Some bakeries also sell a *flûte* which is a smaller, thinner version of the baguette usually made in the old-fashioned way and entirely by hand. You can tell hand made bread because the air holes are uneven and the texture is spongy, but firm at the same time.

All bakeries have *pain de campagne* or country bread, which can range from regular bread dough liberally sprinkled with flour on top, to the use of whole grain flour mixes including rye. A rye bread is a *pain de seigle* and all-grain bread is a *pain au céréale. Pain au levain* is a sort of sourdough bread. Loaves of bread can be sliced, but you have to pay a little more, and, don't expect a bag, either plastic or paper. The bread is usually wrapped in thin waxed paper which is then twisted.

Here is just a short list of some of the exceptional bakeries you can find all over Paris.

Fourth Arrondissement

NATURALLY FERMENTED BREAD
RIOUX ALAIN
35 rue des Deux Ponts, 4th arrondissement
Métro Pont Marie
Open Saturday to Wednesday 6:45 to 8:15
Tel: 01 43 54 57 59

The bread here is naturally fermented, plus they sell pastries, cookies and brownies.

Sixth Arrondissement

AUTHENTIC OLD-FASHIONED BREAD
POILANE
8 rue du Cherche Midi, 6th arrondissement
Métro Sèvres-Babylone
Open Monday to Saturday 7:15 to 8:15
Tel: 01 45 48 42 59

Poilâne was actually one of the first to recreate old-fashioned bread in the 50's. The bread here is whole grain and heavy, baked in enormous rounds in a wood fired oven. You can buy a half or quarter if you want. The current master baker is the son of the founder.

Other location:
49 boulevard de Grenelle, 15th arrondissement, Métro Dupleix, Tel: 01 45 79 11 49, open Tuesday to Sunday 8 to 8.

Seventh Arrondissement

OLD-FASHIONED BREAD
POUJAURAN JEAN-LUC
20 rue Jean Nicot, 7th arrondissement
Métro Latour Maubourg
Open Tuesday to Saturday 8 to 8:30
Tel: 01 47 05 80 88

The selection of old fashioned bread is very good in this well-known bakery. Most of it is made with stone-ground flour and baked in wood-burning ovens.

Ninth Arrondissement

PAST WINNER BEST BAGUETTE OF PARIS
BOULANGERIE HOULBERT
65 rue des Martyrs, 9th arrondissement
Métro Pigalle
Open Monday to Thursday 7 to 2 and 3 to 8, Friday 7 to 2 and 3 to 7:30
Tel: 01 48 78 10 23

A past recipient of the best baguette of Paris award in 1995, the *baguette Martyre d'Or* is still a winner. It has a nutty flavor and a good balance between texture and lightness. The contest is organized by the city of Paris and the judges are food experts and great chefs.

Twentieth Arrondissement

THE BEST BREAD IN PARIS
GANACHAUD
150 rue de Menilmontant, 20th arrondissement
Métro Menilmontant & Bus 96 to Menilmontant-Pelleport stop

Open Wednesday to Saturday 7:30 to 8, Tuesday 2:30 to 8 & Sunday
7:30 to 1
Tel: 01 46 36 13 82

Mr. Ganachaud, Master Baker, created the *flûte Gana* in the 60's based
on a recipe from the turn of the century. It is indeed one of the best, if not
the best breads in Paris. The question is whether you want to come all the
way out to this store to get it. Warning: this bakery is in the outskirts of
Paris far from any convenient Métro (plus you have a substantial walk up
hill or you have to wait for a bus) and it is not cheap—for food fanatics
only. Mr. Ganachaud is retired now and trains other bakers in his technique. I have listed three of them below.

Other locations:
STEFF LE BOULANGER, 123 rue Mouffetard, 5th arrondissement
Métro Place Monge or Censier Daubenton, Open Tuesday to Sunday 7 to
8, Tel: 01 47 07 35 96
STEFF LE BOULANGER, 54 rue de Sèvres, 7th arrondissement
Métro Vaneau, Open Monday to Friday 7 am to 8:30, Saturday 7 to 8,
Tel: 01 47 83 97 12
BOULANGERIE LUPO, 59 rue d'Orsel, 18th arrondissement
Métro Pigalle or Anvers, Open Tuesday to Saturday 6:45 am to 8:15,
Sunday 6:45 to 12:30, Tel: 01 42 23 62 81 (you can see the baker at work
behind a glass window)

PASTRIES

Like the bakeries, one of the great things about Paris is that you can
find excellent pastries just about anywhere. In the following list, I have

included some of the better-known shops or shops that have a little something extra.

First Arrondissement

MONT BLANC & HOT CHOCOLATE
ANGELINA
226 rue de Rivoli, 1st arrondissement
Métro Tuileries
Open every day 11 to 7
Tel: 01 42 60 82 00

Founded in 1903 by René Rumpelmeyer and named after his wife, Angelina is renowned for a pastry called the *Mont Blanc*. This delicacy consists of a meringue topped with whipped cream (*crème chantilly*) plus chestnut cream (Vive la France!). They are also renowned for hot chocolate which you can taste in the *salon de thé* which opens at 9 am.

Other location:
Galeries Lafayette, 40 boulevard Haussmann, 9th arrondissement, Métro Chaussée d'Antin/La Fayette, Tel: 01 42 82 30 32

Sixth Arrondissement

NOT DISCOUNT BUT GO ANYWAY
DALLOYAU
2 Place Edmond Rostand, 6th arrondissementRER Luxembourg
Open every day 8:30 to 8:30 (Salon de Thé 8:30 to 7)
Tel: 01 43 29 31 10

This is one of the best-known pastry shops in Paris, founded in 1802. It's just across from the Luxembourg Gardens, so why not take a café and pastry break after you tour the gardens? In the summer you can sit outside. They also sell gourmet take out food.

Other locations:
25 boulevard des Capucines, 2nd arrondissement, Tel: 01 47 03 47 00
63 rue de Grenelle, 7th arrondissement, Tel: 01 45 49 95 30
101 rue du Faubourg St Honoré, 8th arrondissement, Tel: 01 42 99 90 00
Espace Dalloyau Lafayette Gourmet, 48-52 boulevard Haussmann, 9th arrondissement, Tel: 01 53 20 05 00
69 rue de la Convention, 15th arrondissement, Tel: 01 45 77 84 27

OUTSTANDING PASTRIES
GERARD MULOT
76 rue de Seine, 6th arrondissement
Métro Mabillon or Odéon
Open every day except Wednesday 8 to 8
Tel: 01 43 26 85 77

This is another outstanding pastry shop. Try anything with chocolate, which is their specialty. They also sell a bread called a *bannette* which is made with natural yeast and special flour, made daily.

Seventh Arrondissement

ONE OF THE BEST PASTRY CHEFS IN FRANCE
HEVIN JEAN-PAUL
16 avenue de La Motte Picquet, 7th arrondissement
Métro La Tour Mauberg
Open Tuesday to Saturday 10 to 1:30 and 2:30 to 7
Tel: 01 45 51 77 48

Considering that Mr. Hevin is one of the best pastry chefs in France, the prices are reasonable. Everything is made with fresh ingredients without preservatives or food dyes. Besides pastries they make and sell chocolate available in bags, boxes or fancy containers in wood, porcelain or metal. They also sell jams, preserves, ice cream and sorbet.

Other locations:
231 rue St Honoré, 1st arrondissement, Métro Tuileries, Open every day 10 to 7, Tel: 01 55 35 35 96 (Salon de Thé & Chocolat), Tel: 01 55 35 35 96
3 rue Vavin, 6th arrondissement, Métro Vavin, Open Monday to Saturday 10 to 7:30, Sunday 10 to 2 & 3 to 6, Tel: 01 43 54 09 85

TOP QUALITY PASTRIES
ROLLET-PRADIER
6 rue de Bourgogne, 7th arrondissement
Métro Assemblée Nationale
Open every day 8 to 7:45
Tel: 01 45 51 78 36

Founded in 1859, this is another top pastry shop with reasonable prices considering the quality. They also sell candy, chocolate and gourmet take out food. The *Salon de Thé* is open every day except Sunday until 6.

Eighth Arrondissement

FAMOUS ELEGANT SHOP
LADUREE
75 avenue des Champs Elysées, 8th arrondissement
Métro George V
Open every day 8 to 10
Tel: 01 40 75 08 75

The restaurant/pastry shop recently installed in this location is an offshoot of the original shop on the rue Royale, founded in 1862 as a simple pastry shop. The decor is very elegant, in the style of a private mansion from the end of the 19th century. They're supposed to have the best macaroons in Paris. You may want to take a break in the *Salon de Thé*, open 3 to 7 Monday to Saturday, 3:30 to 7 Sunday.

Other locations:

16 rue Royale, 8th arrondissement, Métro Concorde, Tel: 01 42 60 21 79

Printemps Department Store, 64 boulevard Haussmann, Métro Havre-Caumartin, Tel: 01 42 82 40 10

Franck et Fils Store, 80 rue de Passy, 16th arrondissement, Métro Muette, Tel: 01 44 14 38 80

Ninth Arrondissement

NORTH AFRICAN PASTRIES

ZAZOU FRERES

20 rue du Faubourg Montmartre, 9th arrondissement

Métro Grands Boulevards

Open Sunday to Thursday 8 to 7:30, Friday 7 to sundown

Tel: 01 47 70 81 32

The owners of this bakery are Tunisian Jews and their pastries are outstanding.

Sixteenth Arrondissement

CAKES & PASTRIES

LENOTRE

48 avenue Victor Hugo, 16th arrondissement

Métro Victor Hugo

Open every day 9 to 9
Tel: 01 45 02 21 21

Lenôtre is especially known for their cakes which are practically works of art. Just take a look in the display window before you go into the store! This is definitely a place to splurge (don't we all deserve that every once in awhile?).

Other locations:
15 boulevard de Courcelles, 8th arrondissement, Tel: 01 45 63 87 63
61 rue Lecourbe, 15th arrondissement, Tel: 01 42 73 20 97
44 rue d'Auteuil, 16th arrondissement, Tel: 01 45 24 52 52
121 avenue de Wagram, 17th arrondissement, Tel: 01 47 63 70 30

CLOTHING: NEW

Introduction

First, when shopping for clothing at reduced prices in Paris, you must be vigilant about quality. Examine the garment inside and out, making sure the seams are OK and there are no rips.

You will find the best prices during the months of January/mid-February and mid to late June/July when stores have their bi-annual, government regulated sales which last about 6 weeks. They are not allowed to have a real "sale" during any other period, although they may have promotions of special sale articles from time to time. During the official sale period, items that have been sold previously, have been removed and stored, are then put back with the tag clearly marked both with the original price and the new sale price.

Size conversions:

Women: (dresses & suits)

American	8	10	12	14	16	18
French	38	40	42	44	46	48
British	10	12	14	16	18	20

Men: (suits)				
American	36	38	40	42
French	38	42	46	48
British	36	38	40	42

Men: (shirts)						
American	15	15 1/2	15 3/4	16	16 1/2	17
French	38	39	40	41	42	43
British	15	15 1/2	15 3/4	16	16 1/2	17

A Little More Shopping Vocabulary

TU = *taille unique* (one size fits all)
Size 1 = small, Size 2 = medium, Size 3 = large
Fitting room = *cabine d'essayage*

The French word *fabricant* means manufacturer. In some neighborhoods you'll see a lot of these factory outlets. Most of them only sell wholesale, although a few will sell to individuals. A factory outlet store for the general public is called a *magasin d'usine* which is usually found outside of Paris. In the city, look for the word *stock* in the name of the store, which means the store sells overruns, or new merchandise from past seasons that was never sold. Each brand name(*marque*) handles its own overruns in its own stores. The French verb *brader* means to sell at a discount or to have a clearance sale. So, the word *braderie* means discount or clearance (or rummage) sale.

Shopping Streets

There are several shopping streets with numerous discount stores, one after the other on both sides of the streets. Two of these are the rue d'Alésia in the 14th arrondissement (see Note), Métro Alésia and the rue St Placide in the 6th arrondissement (see Note), Métro Sèvres-Babylone.

First Arrondissement

WILD & CRAZY
FORUM DES JEUNES CREATEURS (men & women)
Shopping Center Forum des Halles, Niveau (Level)–1, Porte Berger or
Porte Rambuteau, 1st arrondissement
Métro Les Halles/RER Les Halles
Open Monday to Saturday 11 to 7
Tel: 01 40 41 00 64

Hidden away on the upper level of the huge underground shopping
center *Les Halles* are a number of stores selling young French designer
clothes. The styles range from unusual to downright weird, and the prices
aren't low, but they are reasonable for designer originals. If you're in the
area it's worth a look to see something really unique. Note that the upper
level is–1 while the lower level is–3.

KNITS
PLUCK IN PLUS (women)
40 rue des Lombards, 1st arrondissement
Métro Les Halles/RER Les Halles
Open Saturday (only)10:30 to 2 & 2:30 to 7
Tel: 01 42 36 82 87

This store specializes in knits, mostly classic designs from the Plück
label. Here is where they discount collections from 2 or 3 years ago. There
are sweaters and pullovers in wool or cotton, and you'll find a lot of stuff
piled up in bins.

KNIT TOPS
KIM (men & women)
91 rue de Rivoli, 1st arrondissement

Métro Louvre Rivoli
Open Monday to Saturday 9:30 to 7, Sunday 10 to 6
Tel: 01 42 60 22 14

This is the place for classic cashmere knit tops. The real bargains are in a pile at the back of the shop.

Second Arrondissement

STYLISH LARGE SIZES
GRIFF' MOD
20 rue des Petits Champs, 2nd arrondissement
Métro Pyramides or Palais Royal
Open Monday to Saturday 10 to 7
Tel: 01 42 97 47 45

Griff' Mod has a special section for large sizes (*rayon special ronde*) with stylish clothing in sizes 46 to 56 (sizes 16 to 26 American; 18 to 28 British).

SUPER DISCOUNT
CHOKI (men & women)
14 rue Notre Dame des Victoires, 2nd arrondissement
Métro Bourse
Open Friday and Saturday 9 to 7
Tel: 01 42 96 48 92

If you're in the neighborhood, it's worth checking out this discounter of name brand skirts, suits, jackets, vests and pants, hidden away in the financial district. They specialize in the brand Weinberg which is known for well-made classic clothes. The prices here very are low, but the selection varies. Be sure to check out the shoes and handbags on the upper floor.

CLASSIC
MANGAS (men)
43 rue Vivienne, 2nd arrondissement
Métro Bourse
Open Monday to Friday 10:30 to 2:30 and 3 to 7, Saturday 10:30 to 2
and 3 to 6:30
Tel: 01 45 08 43 70

In this Spanish chain, you can buy made to order men's clothing for a
reasonable price. You choose the fabric, then they take your measurements
and enter them in a computer which transmits them to the factory. Suits
take 4 weeks, shirts, 2 weeks. In addition, they have ties and coats. They
can even embroider your initials for a small extra fee.

SUPER DISCOUNT & STYLISH
OLIVIER. B (women)
159 rue Montmartre, 2nd arrondissement
Métro Grands Boulevards
Open Monday to Saturday 10:30 to 2 and 3 to 7

This is one of my personal favorites where you can find suits, coats,
blouses, separates, skirts and knit tops. These are medium quality versions
of more expensive stylish clothes. The "look" here is very French.
However, as in most discount stores, sometimes it's really great and sometimes it's not.

Some other locations:
2 rue Croix des Petits Champs, 1st arrondissement, Métro Louvre-Rivoli
21 rue Pierre Lescot, 1st arrondissement, Métro Etienne Marcel
26 passage Choiseul, 2nd arrondissement, Métro Quatre Septembre
86 Rue du Bac, 7th arrondissement, Métro Rue du Bac
26 rue des Belles Feuilles, 16th arrondissement, Métro Victor Hugo

YVES ST LAURENT/CHRISTIAN LACROIX DISCOUNT
MENDES (women)
5 rue d'Uzès, 2nd arrondissement
Métro Grands Boulevards
Open Monday to Thursday 10 to 6:30, Friday & Saturday 10 to 5
Tel: 01 4236 8332

Mendès is the manufacturer of Yves St Laurent's Rive Gauche and Variations collections plus Christian Lacroix and Claude Montana. They have an excellent selection of suits and coats from the previous season at prices up to 50% off retail. Rive Gauche, although ready-to-wear, is only sold in YSL Rive Gauche stores. Originally it was designed by Yves St Laurent himself and is considered to be of higher quality than Variations which is in general distribution. At the time I visited the store, there was no Claude Montana clothing in the store. For those of you who like to sew, at the back of the store there are bolts of left over fabric from the clothes manufacturing. Be sure to look for the sign on the door as there are several entrances to the building. Then, walk up a flight of stairs.

YOUNG LOOK
STOCK KOOKAI (women)
82 rue Réaumur, 2nd arrondissement
Métro Réaumur-Sébastopol
Open Monday to Saturday 10 to 7
Tel: 01 45 08 93 69

Kookaï is a very well known brand for teens and juniors, with styles appealing to the young and thin. They are also known for good quality. In this large store you will find overruns. They carry knit tops, dresses, blouses, skirts, jackets and suits (be prepared for some very short skirts).

MEN'S SHIRTS
LA CHEMISE (men)
64 rue Montmartre, 2nd arrondissement
Métro Les Halles or Bourse/RER Les Halles
Open Monday to Saturday 10:30 to 2 and 3 to 7
Tel: 01 40 39 95 04

They only sell men's shirts in this store, and everything in the store is 100 and 150 FF.

Other locations:
48 rue Mouffetard, 5th arrondissement, Métro Monge, Open Tuesday to Saturday 10:30 to 7:30, Sunday 11 to 7:30, Tel: 01 43 31 48 37
11 boulevard des Batignolles, 8th arrondissement, Métro Place Clichy, Open Tuesday to Saturday 11 to 2 and 3 to 7:30, Tel: 01 42 93 18 34

YOUTH ORIENTED "IN" STYLES
ET VOUS STOCK (men & women)
17 rue de Turbigo, 2nd arrondissement
Métro Etienne Marcel
Open Monday to Saturday noon to 7
Tel: 01 40 13 04 12
Web Site: http://www.etvous.com

The imaginative clothes in this boutique use high quality materials. Designed by Koji Tatsuno, the women's designs appeal to a youth oriented clientele in revolt against the multi-colored fantasies of haute couture. The prices are very good in this store for previous collections with reductions reaching 50% and above.

Third Arrondissement

LOCAL DESIGNER
LESAMIE DE MESAMY (women)
36 rue de Poitou, 3rd arrondissement
Métro Filles du Calvaire
Open Tuesday to Saturday 11 to 7
Tel: 01 42 78 65 35

Hidden away in this industrial neighborhood is this beautiful shop which sells the creations of local designer Elsa Garçon direct to the public. She specializes in knits that are comfortable to wear. The prices are not exactly low, but are good for original designer clothes of high quality. You'll find suits, skirts and knit outfits among other things.

DESIGNER DISCOUNTS
CLAUDE REYNER (men)
92 rue de Turenne, 3rd arrondissement
Métro Filles du Calvaire
Open Monday to Friday 9 to 6, Saturday 10 to 6
Tel: 01 48 87 35 82

Claude Reyner is a wholesaler that sells designer suits (such as Courreges and Daniel Hechter), jackets, sweaters and pullovers at a reduced price.

DISCOUNT DESIGNER
L'HABILLEUR (women & men)
44 rue de Poitou, 3rd arrondissement
Métro Filles du Calvaire
Open Monday to Saturday 11 to 8
Tel: 01 48 87 77 12

The quality varies at this store for overbuys and last year's collection designer clothes from France, England and other European countries. You will, however, occasionally find runway models and prototypes at major reductions. Among the designers is John Richmond at up to 50% off. If you're in the neighborhood, it's worth checking out for coats, suits, pants, jackets, shoes and so on.

COATS & JACKETS
IMEX (women)
8 rue des Francs Bourgeois, 3rd arrondissement
Métro St Paul
Open Tuesday to Friday 10:30 to 7 , Monday 2:30 to 7, Saturday 11 to 7
Tel: 01 48 87 14 76

This store, hidden at the back of a courtyard, sells jackets and coats at medium high prices, but they are a good value for the quality. They also sell designer buttons and ribbons.

Fourth Arrondissement

SPORTS CLOTHES & JEANS
DANIEL (women)
42 rue St Antoine, 4th arrondissement
Métro St Paul or Bastille
Open Tuesday to Friday 10:30 to 7:30, Saturday 10 to 7:30, Monday 2 to 7:30
Tel: 01 48 04 97 53

Daniel has a great selection of knit tops, plus pants, jackets and loads of French jeans in the basement. Prices are reasonable.

Other locations:
9 rue Gay Lussac, 5th arrondissement, RER Luxembourg

DESIGNER
STUDIO LOLITA (women)
2 bis rue des Rosiers, 4th arrondissement
Métro St Paul
Open Tuesday to Saturday 10:30 to 1:30 and 2:30 to 7
Tel: 01 48 87 09 67

Lolita Lempicka is a designer well worth knowing for her very feminine and lively designs. You can ignore the high-priced store on the corner of rue des Rosiers and rue Pavée and turn right half a block to find this small shop that sells last year's fashions. They mainly sell dresses and suits, but it depends on the season. The prices are reasonable for designer original clothing.

STYLISH
NINA JACOB (women)
23 rue des Francs Bourgeois, 4th arrondissement
Métro St Paul
Open every day 10 to 7
Tel: 01 42 77 41 20

Nina Jacob is worth checking out if you are in the neighborhood. You'll find stylish clothing, including a lot of knits (using a blend of natural fibers and synthetics). The selection includes suits, sweaters, coats, skirts, jackets and pants. The prices are mid-range.

ITALIAN FASHION
TUTTI QUANTI (men & women)
45 rue des Francs Bourgeois, 4th arrondissement

Métro St Paul
Open Monday to Saturday 1 to 7, Sunday 2 to 7
Tel: 01 48 87 65 18

This store sells discounted Italian clothes including a good selection of knit tops, plus suits and pants. If you are traveling to Italy in the near future, you can definitely skip this store! But, if not, why not check it out. Just tell your friends that you bought the clothes in Paris, which is the truth, isn't it?

DISCOUNT DESIGNER
GAMMES DE... (women)
17 rue du Temple, 4th arrondissement
Métro Hôtel de Ville
Open Monday to Saturday 10 to 7
Tel: 01 48 04 57 57

Here you'll find designer clothes at a reduced price, especially Guy Laroche. The selection includes suits, dresses, knit tops, jackets, coats and blouses.

DESIGNER
AZZEDINE ALAIA
18 rue de la Verrerie, 4th arrondissement
Métro Hôtel de Ville
Open Tuesday to Saturday 10 to 1 and 2 to 7
Tel: 01 42 72 19 19

In an unmarked courtyard, behind anonymous glass windows resides the past collections of this Tunisian born designer. You'll find unique dresses, pants, knit tops and some shoes at up to 50% off. The styles are definitely youth oriented and sizes are limited. Prices, though reduced, are still in the high range.

Sixth Arrondissement

Note: The rue St Placide in a 2-block stretch from rue de Sèvres to rue de Vaugirard is a solid mass of discount stores, on both sides of the street. Many of the stores sell low-quality goods for low prices, so you'll have to pay a lot of attention to the quality. I've listed 3 stores on the street that stand out, but the best technique is to start out at one end, go down one side and back on the other, visiting each store. The closest Métros are Sèvres-Babylone or St Placide.

NAME BRANDS
MOUTON A CINQ PATTES (men and women)
8, 14 and 18 rue St Placide, 6th arrondissement
Métro Sèvres Babylone
Open Monday 2 to 7:30, Tuesday to Friday 10:30 to 7:30, Sunday 11 to 8 (closed 2 to 3 every day)
Tel: 01 45 44 83 25

This is the real thing—piles in bins and racks stuffed with name brands at discount prices. But, the selection is uneven—sometimes good, sometimes bad. So, don't go out of your way to find this shop, but if you're in the neighborhood it wouldn't hurt to check it out. They sell men's shirts, pants, vests and jackets plus women's skirts, suits, pants and blouses, among other things.

Other locations:
15 rue Vieille du Temple, 4th arrondissement, Métro St Paul, or Hotel de Ville, Tel: 01 42 71 86 30

138 boulevard St Germain, 6th arrondissement, Métro Odéon, Tel: 01 45 48 86 26
L'Annexe, 48 rue St Placide, 6th arrondissement, Métro St Placide (men), Tel: 01 45 48 82 85
19 rue Grégoire de Tours, 6th arrondissement, Métro Odéon, Tel: 01 43 29 73 56
130 avenue Victor Hugo, 16th arrondissement, Métro Pompe, Tel: 01 47 55 42 25

TAILORED
BOUTIQUE STOCK CAROLL (women)
26, 30 & 51 rue St Placide, 6th arrondissement
Métro Sèvres-Babylone
Open Monday to Saturday 10 to 7
Tel: 01 45 48 83 66

Caroll is a line of clothing that has a tailored look, using synthetic fabrics and blends. This store sells the overruns, and the prices are low.

Other location:
91 rue St Dominique, 7th arrondissement, Métro Latour Maubourg, Tel: 01 44 18 08 76

AGES 0 TO 14
DU PAREIL AU MEME (children)
14 rue St Placide, 6th arrondissement
Métro Sèvres-Babylone
Open Monday to Saturday 10 to 7
Tel: 01 45 44 04 40

One of the best chains in Paris for babies' and children's clothes, Du Pareil au Même is known for high quality at the low prices. They have their own team of in-house designers who create colorful and comfortable designs for ages 0 to 14. So, it's constantly filled with French mothers seeking good buys and is absolutely packed in September just before the annual return to school. Du Pareil au Même Maison specializes in infants and up to one year old. They sell, besides baby clothes, toys, decoration and furniture for children's rooms (including wall paper), birth presents, baby carriages, baby bottles and supplies, etc.

Other locations:

168 boulevard Saint Germain, 6th arrondissement, Métro Mabillon, Tel: 01 46 33 89 88

(Maison) 7 rue Vavin, 6th arrondissement, Métro Vavin, Tel: 01 43 54 12 34

15-17 rue des Mathurins, 8th arrondissement, Métro Havre-Caumartin, Tel: 01 42 66 93 80

(Maison) 23 rue des Mathurins, 8th arrondissement, Métro Havre Caumartin, Tel: 01 47 42 63 32

24 rue du Mogador, 9th arrondissement, Métro Trinité, Tel: 01 42 82 13 33

122 rue du Faubourg Saint Antoine, 12th arrondissement, Métro Ledru Rollin, Tel: 01 43 43 96 01

(Maison) 120 rue du Faubourg Saint Antoine, Métro Ledru Rollin, Tel: 01 43 43 44 99

165 rue du Château des Rentiers, 13th arrondissement, Métro Nationale, Tel: 01 45 83 03 08

10 boulevard Brune, 14th arrondissement, Métro Porte de Vanves, Tel: 01 45 39 65 95

6 rue de l'Ouest, 14th arrondissement, Métro Gaîté, Tel: 01 43 20 59 57

(Maison) 15 rue de l'Ouest, 14th arrondissement, Métro Gaîté, Tel: 01 43 21 46 21

59 rue du Commerce, 15th arrondissement, Métro Emile Zola, Tel: 01 45 75 93 40

(Maison) 27 rue du Commerce, 15th arrondissement, Métro Emile Zola, Tel: 01 45 75 93 40

3 rue de la Pompe, 16th arrondissement, Métro La Muette, Tel: 01 42 24 82 84

97 avenue Victor Hugo, 16th arrondissement, Métro Victor Hugo, Tel: 01 47 27 48 10

(Maison) 111 avenue Victor Hugo, 16th arrondissement, Métro Victor Hugo, Tel: 01 47 27 48 10

16 avenue Niel, 17th arrondissement, Métro Ternes, Tel: 01 47 66 56 52

(Maison) 49 avenue des Ternes, 17th arrondissement, Métro Ternes, Tel: 01 45 74 08 60

128 boulevard de Courcelles, 17th arrondissement, Métro Ternes, Tel: 01 47 66 03 31

38 rue du Poteau, 18th arrondissement, Métro Jules Joffrin, Tel: 01 42 54 71 61

27 avenue Secretan, 19th arrondissement
Métro Jaurès, Tel: 01 40 40 76 76

209 boulevard Davout, 20th arrondissement, Métro Porte de Bagnolet, Tel: 01 43 64 95 10

AGES 14 TO 20
SERELOU (teens)
7 rue St Placide, 6th arrondissement
Métro Sèvres-Babylone
Open Monday to Saturday 10 to 7
Tel: 01 40 49 00 33

Owned by the same company as Du Pareil au Même, Serelou is a great store for teen and youth oriented adult clothes including pants, sweats, separates and a great collection of socks. Prices are very reasonable.

Other locations:

122 rue du Faubourg St Antoine, 12th arrondissement, Métro Faidherbe-Chaligny, Tel: 01 43 43 96 01

18-20 rue du Commerce, 15th arrondissement, Métro La Motte Picquet Grenelle, Tel: 01 45 75 65 11

AGES 0 TO 14
TOUT COMPTE FAIT...(children)
31 rue St Placide, 6th arrondissement
Métro Saint Placide
Open Monday to Saturday 9:30 to 7
Tel: 01 42 22 45 64

This is another children's and infant's clothing store, with very cute designs and reasonable prices. It's similar to Du Pareil au Même mentioned above, but with different styles. Between these two stores, you have a very wide choice.

Other locations:

170 rue du Temple, 3rd arrondissement, Métro Temple, Tel: 01 40 27 00 42

69 boulevard St Michel, 5th arrondissement, RER Luxembourg, Tel: 01 46 33 52 54

62 rue de la Chaussée d'Antin, 9th arrondissement, Métro Chaussée d'Antin, Tel: 01 48 74 16 54

128 rue du Faubourg St Antoine, 12th arrondissement, Métro Faidherbe Chaligny, Tel: 01 43 46 94 32

101 bis rue d'Alésia, 14th arrondissement, Métro Alésia, Tel: 01 45 39 84 85

63 rue du Commerce, 15th arrondissement, Métro Commerce, Tel: 01 48 28 00 66

334 rue de Vaugirard, 15th arrondissement, Métro Convention, Tel: 01 45 30 16 36

115 avenue Victor Hugo, 16th arrondissement, Métro Victor Hugo, Tel: 01 47 55 63 36

11 rue de Lévis, 17th arrondissement, Métro Villiers, Tel: 01 43 87 19 14

72 rue Ordener at the Square Clignancourt, 18th arrondissement, Métro Jules Joffrin, Tel: 01 42 64 00 21

23 avenue Sécrétan, 19th arrondissement, Métro Jaurès, Tel: 01 42 02 08 19

116 rue de Belleville, 20th arrondissement, Métro Jourdain, Tel: 01 43 66 42 44

DISCOUNT DESIGNER & NAME BRANDS
STOCK GRIFFES (women)
25 rue Dauphine, 6th arrondissement
Métro Odéon
Open Tuesday to Saturday 11 to 7:30
Tel: 01 43 29 20 47

In Stock Griffes, you will find a good selection of designer knit tops, suits, skirts, jackets, coats and knit outfits at reduced prices. Designers can include Odile Lançon, Lilith, Popy Moreni and Irina Gregorovitch among others.

Other locations:
17 rue Vieille du Temple, 3rd arrondissement, Métro Hôtel de Ville or St Paul, Open 10:30 to 7:30, Tel: 01 48 04 82 34

1 rue des Trois Frères, 18th arrondissement, Métro Abbesses, Open 10 to 7, Tel: 01 42 55 42 49

48 rue d'Orsel, 18th arrondissement, Métro Pigalle or Anvers, Tel: 01 42 52 58 60

SPORTS CLOTHES
CLEF DES MARQUES (women & children)
126 boulevard Raspail, 6th arrondissement
Métro Vavin
Open Tuesday to Friday 10 to 2 and 3 to 7 , Saturday 10 to 1 and 2 to 7 , Monday 12:30 to 7
Tel: 01 45 49 31 00

You'll find lots of sports clothes in this discount shop. The really good buys are way in the back, which is also where you'll find the children's clothes. They sell skirts, blouses, pants, sweaters, jackets, raincoats and some lingerie.

Other locations:
20 place du Marché St Honoré, 1st arrondissement, Métro Tuileries or Pyramides, Tel: 01 47 03 90 40
99 rue St Dominique, 7th arrondissement, Métro Latour Maubourg, Tel: 01 47 05 04 55
86 rue du Faubourg St Antoine, 11th arrondissement, Métro Ledru Rollin, Tel: 01 40 01 95 15

LARGE SIZES
GRANDES TAILLES (women)
46 rue Notre Dame des Champs, 6th arrondissement
Métro Vavin
Open Monday to Saturday 10 to 7
Tel: 01 42 22 03 03

If you're looking for large sizes, you should check out this store. They have a small but stylish selection of clothing with flattering lines for larger women. The prices are medium to high.

Eighth Arrondissement

CLASSIC

ADOLFO DOMINGUEZ (men & women)
24 rue Royale, 8th arrondissement
Métro Madeleine or Concorde
Open Tuesday to Saturday 10:30 to 7 , Monday 12 to 7
Tel: 01 44 58 96 10

The prices are mid-range, but the quality is high in this Spanish chain. The styles are classic with clean lines and natural fabrics in neutral shades. You will find coats, jackets and outfits for both sexes and pants suits and dresses for women. Women's clothing is upstairs.

Other locations:
2 rue Catinat, 1st arrondissement, Métro Palais Royal, Tel: 01 42 60 09 94
Le Carrousel du Louvre Shopping Center, 99 rue de Rivoli, 1st arrondissement, Métro Palais Royal, Tel: 01 42 60 30 11 (closed Tuesday)

YOUNG INTERNATIONAL STYLE

ZARA (men, women & children)
44 avenue des Champs Elysées, 8th arrondissement
Métro Franklin D. Roosevelt
Open Monday to Saturday 10 to 7:30
Tel: 01 45 61 52 80

Zara is a Spanish chain known for it's creative window displays and store interior design. The clothes are trendy young European styles using somber colors and straight lines. The chain economizes by using a lot of synthetic fabrics, though occasionally you will find 100% cotton knits. You can expect to find women's dresses, separates and knit tops. The prices are mid-range.

Other locations:

128 rue de Rivoli, 1st arrondissement, Métro Châtelet, Tel: 01 44 82 64 00 (men, women & children)

Forum des Halles, 5 Passage des Verrières, 1st arrondissement, Métro/RER Les Halles, Tel: 01 55 34 98 51 (women)

45 rue de Rennes, 6th arrondissement, Métro St Germain, Tel: 01 44 39 03 50 (men & women)

38 avenue des Champs Elysées, 8th arrondissement, Métro Franklin Roosevelt, Tel: 01 56 59 10 (women)

8 boulevard des Capucines/2 rue Halévy, 9th arrondissement, Métro Opéra, Tel: 01 44 71 90 90 (men, women & children)

Le Printemps, 64 boulevard Haussmann, 9th arrondissement, Métro Havre-Caumartin, Tel: 01 42 82 49 56 (women)

Passage du Havre, 107 rue St Lazare, 9th arrondissement, Métro St Lazare, Tel: 01 53 32 82 95 (women)

Centre Commercial Montparnasse, 15th arrondissement

33 avenue du Maine, Métro Montparnasse-Bienvenüe, Tel: 01 40 64 04 40 (men & women)

53 rue de Passy, 16th arrondissement, Métro Passy or La Muette, Tel: 01 45 25 07 00 (women)

28-32 avenue Victor Hugo, 16th arrondissement, Métro Victor Hugo, Tel: 01 53 64 00 20 (women)

DISCOUNT DESIGNER
TRENTE-HUIT FRANCOIS Ier, COTE JARDIN (women and men)
38 rue François Ier, 8th arrondissement
Métro Franklin D. Roosevelt
Open Monday to Saturday 10 to 7
Tel: 01 47 20 73 13

On the ground and first floors of this large store, you'll find an excellent selection of designer clothes from the last few seasons. On the second floor

is men's clothes. The styles are classic and the prices are good considering the designers represented. On the first floor is a room with used women's designer clothes as well.

Ninth Arrondissement

CLASSIC
COMPTOIR DES CHEMISES (men)
10 rue de Sèze, 9th arrondissement
Métro Madeleine
Open Tuesday to Saturday 10:30 to 7 , Monday 12 to 7
Tel: 01 47 42 99 73

The clothing in this store is manufactured in their own factory in France. You'll find shirts, pants, sweaters, and ties at discounted prices.

DISCOUNT DESIGNER
ANNEXE DES CRÉATEURS (men & women)
19 rue Godot de Mauroy, 9th arrondissement
Métro Madeleine
Open Monday to Saturday 10:30 to 7
Tel: 01 42 65 46 40

Annexe des Créateurs is a great store (2 stores actually, 1 for evening wear and the other for day wear) which sells designer label clothes at a discount. The owner selects everything personally in small batches, paying attention to current fashion trends. Sometimes you can find terrific bargains. When I was there I spotted Versace and Christian LaCroix among others. The selection generally includes dresses, suits, blouses and shirts, coats, skirts, pants and some purses. Sometimes they even have a bargain basement.

THE IKEA OF CLOTHING STORES
H & M (men and women)
Passage du Havre, 107 rue St Lazare, 9th arrondissement
Métro St Lazare (exit #3),
Open Monday to Saturday 10 to 7:30
Tel: 01 53 32 87 97
Web Site: http://www.hm.com

Welcome to the Ikea of clothing stores in this popular chain, founded in Sweden in 1947, where you'll find basic quality for low, low prices. The styles are geared for an age range of 25 to 35, (you can see this when you look at the micro-skirts), but they also have some classic styles that can be worn by anyone, including pretty dresses. Generally, the clothes are designed in an international "basic" style. The selection of 100% cotton knit tops is especially good, as is men's shirts. There is also a good selection of inexpensive women's bags and jewelry, especially silvery necklaces and earrings.

Other locations:
120 rue de Rivoli, 1st arrondissement, Métro Châtelet, Tel: 01 55 34 96 86 (men, women, teens & children)
Shopping Center Forum des Halles, Niveau (Level) -3 & -2, Porte Lescot (facing FNAC), 1st arrondissement, Métro Les Halles/RER Châtelet Les Halles

Tenth Arrondissement
DESIGNER
AFTER BEACH (women)
12 rue Bouchardon, 10th arrondissement
Métro Strasbourg-St Denis
Tel: 01 42 45 18 00

Open Tuesday to Friday 10 to 12 and Wednesday and Friday, 4 to 7 when there is somebody to mind the store! Definitely call ahead to make sure someone will be there.

This store sells last year's models of Ronald Fera. Don't be discouraged by the industrial neighborhood—this is a jewel of a store. The prices are very reasonable for high-quality clothes

Eleventh Arrondissement

DESIGNER/SEXY KNIT DRESSES
CORINNE COBSON
166 rue de la Roquette, Métro Voltaire
Open Monday to Friday 10 to 1 & 2 to 6 (call ahead to confirm)
Tel: 01 40 24 21 21

Known for sexy and flattering knit dresses and tops, Corinne Cobson sells off pieces from end of the season and past seasons in this space for up to 50% off retail price. I say space because it's really an extension of her workshop where they put together the new collections. So, while the room might be plain, the clothes are just the opposite. Be warned that you have to be on the thin side (putting is mildly) to look good in these clothes! It's best to call ahead because they shut down occasionally when they have models in for fittings, press showings, etc. Generally, you will find, besides the sexy knit dresses and tops, knit skirts and pants plus non-knit jackets, pants and whatever else is left over from previous collections.

FABULOUS DESIGNER
ATELIER 33 (women)
33 rue du Faubourg St Antoine, 11th arrondissement
Métro Bastille

Open Monday to Saturday 10 to 7:30
Tel: 01 43 40 61 63

The fabrics and designs in this store are of the highest quality. So, although the prices are not low, it's still a bargain for unique creations by designer Henry Leparque. You will find 2 floors of suits (some of the most original designs I have seen), plus jackets, skirts, pants and sweaters.

UNIQUE DESIGNER
OGIVE (women)
38 rue Faidherbe, 11th arrondissement
Métro Charonne
Open Monday to Saturday 11:30 to 7:30
Tel: 01 43 79 64 66

The clothes in this small boutique are not classic French, but rather original designs in high-quality fabrics which are comfortable to wear and have very flowing lines. You'll find jumpers, dresses, pants, jackets and knit tops. The prices are medium high, but it's a good value for original designs created by the two women who own the shop.

Other location:
11 rue Oberkampf, 11th arrondissement, Métro Oberkampf, Tel: 01 47 00 71 76

Fourteenth Arrondissement

Note: The rue d'Alésia from avenue du Général Leclerc to no. 149 is a grouping of some great discount shops in Paris. I have listed only a few highlights; there were too many stores to list them all. The best technique, as for the rue St Placide, is to start at one end, walk down one side of the street and back down the other, visiting all the stores. The quality tends to be better on the rue d'Alésia than on the rue St Placide, so the prices are a bit higher.

NAME BRAND
CACHAREL STOCK (men, women, little girls)
114 rue d'Alésia, 14th arrondissement
Métro Alésia
Open Monday to Saturday 10 to 7
Tel: 01 45 42 53 04

Here you will find last year's Cacharel at reduced prices. They sell suits, blouses and shirts, knit tops, pants and dresses.

NAME BRAND
MAJESTIC BY CHEVIGNON (men)
122 rue d'Alésia, 14th arrondissement
Métro Alésia
Open Tuesday to Saturday 10 to 7 , Monday 2 to 7
Tel: 45 43 40 25

If you like Chevignon, don't miss this store where they sell Chevignon jackets, sweats and sweaters at reduced prices.

DESIGNER
STOCK 2 (men, women, children)
92 rue d'Alésia, 14th arrondissement
Métro Alésia
Open Monday to Saturday 10 to 7:30
Tel: 01 45 41 65 57

Daniel Hechter overruns are sold at prices that are a good value for designer clothes. The store is large, and in the men's department, you'll find suits, ties, jackets, socks, coats and sweaters. The women's styles include coats, suits, knit tops, blouses, dresses and pants.

DESIGNER
S.R. STORE (women)
64 rue d'Alésia, 14th arrondissement
Métro Alésia
Open Wednesday to Saturday 10 to 7 (11 to 7 Tuesday)
Tel: 01 43 95 06 13

S.R. stands for Sonia Rykiel, and here you'll find her designs from last season. There are beautiful suits, pants and knit outfits, all at reduced prices.

Other location:
82 rue de Lévis, 17th arrondissement, Métro Villiers, Tel: 01 43 80 00 67

COMFORTABLE AND STYLISH
REGINA RUBENS STOCK (women)
88 rue d'Alésia, 14th arrondissement
Métro Alésia
Open Monday to Saturday 10 to 7
Tel: 01 40 44 90 05

When her marriage ended in divorce, Regina Rubens took her life in hand and created her clothing line and boutiques. The styles are modern and comfortable using long clean lines and high quality fabrics. Thankfully, her aim is to design for real women, not models! This store sells previous collections at a reduction of about 30%.

KNIT TOPS
TRICOTS ARLEQUIN (women)
222 avenue du Maine, 14th arrondissement

Métro Alésia
Open Tuesday to Saturday 10:30 to 2 and 3 to 7:30
Tel: 01 45 41 22 47

This store sells beautiful knit tops in natural fibers and blends. The prices range from medium to low.

Fifteenth Arrondissement

NAME BRANDS
LE JARDIN DES MARQUES (men and women)
17 bis boulevard Victor, 15th arrondissement
Métro Porte de Versailles
Open Monday to Saturday 10 to 7 (closed Monday morning)
Tel: 01 45 33 62 02

If you're in the neighborhood you might want to check out this small discount store. Women's clothing include suits, pants, skirts and blouses. Men's clothing includes shirts, jackets and sportswear.

Sixteenth Arrondissement

STYLISH BUT SYNTHETIC MATERIALS
KESAKO (women)
36 rue de Passy, 16th arrondissement
Métro Passy or La Muette
Open Monday to Saturday 10 to 7:30
Tel: 01 42 88 09 98

The clothes here are stylish, but made of synthetic materials, which is why the prices are very reasonable. If you select carefully you can find real bargains.

Seventeenth Arrondissement

ITALIAN KNITS
GOOD DEAL (men & women)
6 rue des Colonels Renard, 17th arrondissement
Métro Argentine
Open Tuesday to Saturday 11 to 2 & 3 to 7
Tel: 01 45 74 30 24

I saw a lot of Italian knits in this discount store which sells last year's collections from the boutique Victoire located on the Place des Victoires (which is one of the most up-scale shopping areas). You'll also find a lot of men's shirts and pants plus women's skirts and pants, besides the knit tops.

Eighteenth Arrondissement

ORIGINAL DESIGNS
PATRICIA LOUISOR (women)
16 rue Houdon, 18th arrondissement
Métro Abbesses
Open every day 11:30 to 8
Tel: 01 42 62 10 42

Patricia Louisor is called a young designer (*jeune createur*) because her designs are original, but she does not do haute couture. Her styles are youth oriented and comfortable using a lot of synthetic knits. The prices are reasonable considering the originality of the designs.

"IN" DESIGNS
RALPH KEMP (women)
18 rue Houdon, 18th arrondissement
Métro Abbesses

Open Tuesday to Sunday noon to 8
Tel: 01 46 06 51 05

Right next door to Patricia Louisor, Ralph Kemp is another young designer who is very "in" at the moment. In this boutique they sell off the end of series, previous collections and a few prototypes from fashion shows. The clothes are stylish and use high quality fabrics. The prices are good for the level of workmanship and the original designs.

CREATIVE
NID D'ABEILLE (women)
22 rue Houdon, 18th arrondissement
Métro Abbesses
Open Tuesday to Saturday noon to 8
Tel: 01 42 59 59 48

The third store in a row along the rue Houdon, Nid d'Abeille sells designs by an Indian designer using clean lines and lovely fabrics. The prices are good considering the originality and workmanship of the clothes.

CLASSIC
BOUTIQUE LA CITADELLE (women)
1 rue des Trois Frères, 18th arrondissement
Métro Pigalle or Anvers
Open Monday to Saturday 11 to 8, Sunday 11 to 7 (in August, 11 to 1:30, 2:30 to 8, closed Sunday)
Tel: 01 42 52 21 56

What you have here is a small collection of classic clothes including suits, skirts, dresses, and knit tops. The prices are medium.

UNIQUE DESIGNS
HEAVEN (women)
83 rue des Martyrs, 18th arrondissement
Métro Pigalle or Anvers
Open Monday 2 to 7:30, Tuesday to Saturday 11 to 7:30
Tel: 01 44 92 92 92

In this store you'll find unique designs and fantasy jewelry at reasonable prices.

SUPER DISCOUNT
LA PETITE BERTHE (men & women)
7 place St Pierre and 16 rue Seveste, 18th arrondissement
Métro Anvers
Open Monday to Saturday 9:15 to 6:30 (closed Monday morning)
Tel: 01 46 06 52 50

The best bargains in this store are actually outside the store in the bins. You can find sweats, socks, knit tops and men's shirts. The quality is medium and the prices are low. If you like to sew, this is right across the square from the St Pierre fabric store.

SUPER DISCOUNT
SYMPA (men, women & children)
68 boulevard Rochechouart, 18th arrondissement
Métro Anvers
Open Monday to Saturday 10:15 to 7:30
Tel: 01 42 54 26 97

This store is a zoo on Saturday, so if you are at all claustrophobic (like me), go during the week! I might also add that you must be willing to sort through bins if you want to find some bargains. Basically you will find medium to low-quality goods for low prices, but if you're in the area, come on down!

Other locations:
1 bis, 2, 3, 7 rue de Steinkerque, 18th arrondissement, Métro Anvers (baby clothes)
4, 16, 18, 24 rue d'Orsel, 18th arrondissement, Métro Anvers (at 24—shoes)

SUPER PLUS DISCOUNT
TATI (men, women & children)
2 to 42 boulevard Rochechouart, 18th arrondissement
Métro Barbés-Rochechouart
Open Monday to Saturday 9:15 to 7
Tel: 01 42 55 13 09
Web Site: http://www.tati.fr

What I just said for Sympa goes double (or triple) for Tati. This is super discount, Paris style (with a little North African/African ambiance thrown in). Be aware that the quality varies (I have to admit that certain items have been known to fall apart after being washed!) So, take one deep breath before entering the store, and be prepared to be bumped and jostled. The bins outside are an adventure too.

Other location:
13 place de la République, 3rd arrondissement, Métro République, Tel: 01 48 87 72 81

EXCEPTIONAL CLASSIC
CREATIONS MICHEL COLIN (men)
15 rue du Ruisseau, 18th arrondissement
Métro Lamarck-Caulaincourt

Open Monday to Saturday 8:30 to 6
Tel: 01 46 06 30 00

You've got to be able to navigate a lot of steps to get to this manufacturer's outlet near Montmartre. If you can do it, it's worth it. This is a huge warehouse full of high-quality classic men's suits and coats at reduced prices. For those who sew, there are remnants in the front and in the back, and there are a few women's suits and separates.

Twentieth Arrondissement

CLASSIC
SCALP (women)
12 boulevard de Charonne, 20th arrondissement
Métro/RER Nation
Open Tuesday to Saturday 10 to 7 (11 to 7 Monday)
Tel: 01 43 73 10 85

You'll find an excellent selection of end of series Weill in this large store. They sell suits, jackets, coats, skirts and pants in styles that tend to be classic.

Other locations:
188 avenue du Maine, 14th arrondissement, Métro Alésia, Tel: 01 45 40 44 93
102 rue St Charles, 15th arrondissement, Métro Charles Michels, Tel: 01 45 77 13 09

CLOTHING: USED

Introduction

There is a substantial market in Paris for used designer clothing. This category includes both haute couture designers who also create ready to wear collections and name designers who do not create haute couture, but are, nevertheless, very well known. They are called *créateurs* in French and include names such as Agnès B, Azzedine Alaïa, Kenzo, Sonia Rykiel and Corinne Cobson, among others.

The market is big because many French women want to be at the height of fashion at all times. So, they sell off their designer clothes as soon as the season changes, even if they have hardly worn them. The stores which sell these clothes on consignment are known as *dépôt-ventes*. The prices are not low, but are much less than brand new. If your budget permits, it's worth checking out some of these stores for high fashion, at moderate to high prices instead of stratospheric. Most of these stores are very fashion conscious themselves and will only carry items that are in excellent condition and *à la mode* (i.e. in fashion!). Be aware that with this kind of merchandise there are no returns or exchanges.

There are also stores that sell *fripes* or secondhand clothes that are not designer. The best known is Guerrisol, listed in the 17th arrondissement.

First Arrondissement

LUXURIOUS
WK ACCESSOIRES (women)
5 rue du Marché St Honoré, 1st arrondissement
Métro Tuileries
Open Tuesday to Saturday 11 to 7
Tel: 01 40 20 99 76

Accessoires means accessories and that's what you'll find in this posh store. This includes handbags, shoes, jewelry plus some clothes such as suits, coats and skirts, all from major designers such as Dior, Chanel, Hermès and Vuitton.

Second Arrondissement

LARGE SELECTION
LA MARELLE (women and children)
21/25 Galerie Vivienne, 2nd arrondissement
Métro Bourse or Palais Royal
Open Monday to Friday 10:30 to 6:30 and Saturday 2 to 6
Tel: 01 42 60 08 19

A large selection of name designer and haute couture clothes fills this store in the charming Galerie Vivienne. You will find separates, suits, coats and even shoes among other items.

GOOD PRICES
GUERRIDA (women)
47 avenue de l'Opéra, 2nd arrondissement
Métro Opéra
Open every day 10 to 7

Only a stone's throw from glamorous Place de l'Opéra is this used clothing store which sells the high end of Guerrisol, famous for recycled old clothes sold at rock bottom prices (see listing in 17th arrondissement). Here are the finer articles including fur coats, blouses, jackets, separates and jewelry, among other things. It's definitely worth taking a look if you're in the area. The prices are very reasonable, but inspect carefully before you buy as there may be spots or other flaws.

Fourth Arrondissement

SMALL BUT GOOD SELECTION
AUTOUR D'ELLES (women)
20 rue des Tournelles, 4th arrondissement
Métro Bastille
Open Tuesday to Saturday 11 to 7 and Sunday 2 to 7
Tel: 01 42 72 90 35

The prices are good and clearly indicated in this small but select store. Haute couture designer items are mixed in with name designer clothes, all of high quality. You will also find some accessories such as shoes, belts and handbags.

"IN" DESIGNERS
ALTERNATIVES (men & women)
18 rue du Roi de Sicile, 4th arrondissement
Métro St Paul
Open Tuesday to Saturday 11 to 1 & 2:30 to 7
Tel: 01 42 78 31 50

Most of the clothing in this small store has been left by models or fashion reporters. So, you can count on the latest styles and "in" designers such as Matsuda, Yamamoto and Michel Klein. There are men's suits, and women's separates and jackets. It's definitely worth checking out if you're in the neighborhood.

Sixth Arrondissement

SMALL SIZES
AU GRE DU VENT (women)
10 rue des Quatre Vents, 6th arrondissement
Métro Odéon
Open Monday 2:30 to 7 and Tuesday to Saturday 10:30 to 7
Tel: 01 44 07 28 73

If you wear small sizes, this is the store for you. The prices are very good, and you will find an excellent selection of suits, separates, coats and so on. Many of the designs are youth oriented designer names such as Angès B.

CHANEL & HERMES
CATHERINE B. (women)
1 rue Guisarde, 6th arrondissement
Métro Odéon
Open Monday 2:30 to 8, Tuesday to Saturday 10:30 to 8
Tel: 01 43 54 74 18

If you like Chanel, this minuscule shop is the place for you. Mme. Catherine B. has even been on a French TV magazine show about the used clothing market in Paris. She buys directly from wealthy French women instead of selling on consignment. You'll also find Hermès clothing and scarves.

NAME DESIGNERS
MISENTROC (men and women)

63 rue Notre Dame des Champs and 15 rue Vavin, 6th arrondissement
Métro Vavin
Open Tuesday to Friday 10:30 to 1 and 2 to 7
Tel: 01 46 33 03 67

The boutique on rue Vavin is more youth oriented while the one on rue Notre Dame des Champs is more classic. In one or the other you'll find clothing by Yves St Laurent along with Agnès B, in addition to Hermès scarves. It's mainly ready to wear, with an occasional true haute couture item.

LARGE AND WELL ORGANIZED
CHERCHEMINIPPES (men, women and children)
102, 109, 110, and 111 rue du Cherche Midi, 6th arrondissement
Métro Duroc
Open Monday to Saturday 10:30 to 7
Tel: 01 42 22 45 23

Take advantage of 4 stores, each with a different specialty: women's ready-to-wear, women's name and designer, men's, and children's clothes. The stores are spacious and well organized with a good selection. You can even find housewares in the women's ready-to-wear store.

Seventh Arrondissement

GOOD NEIGHBORHOOD/SMALL SIZES
DEPOT-VENTE MARIE J.L. (women)
5 rue Auguereau, 7th arrondissement
Métro Ecole Militaire
Open Tuesday to Saturday 10:30 to 7
Tel: 01 45 55 81 25

This store is situated in a very good neighborhood, so the selection is excellent with a lot of designer clothes in mint condition. The one negative is that they only carry small sizes.

SMALL BUT VARIED
DE FIL EN TROC (women)
1 avenue de La Motte Picquet, 7th arrondissement
Métro Latour Maubourg
Open Tuesday to Saturday 10:30 to 7
Tel: 01 47 05 60 13

The collection here is small but varied. Unfortunately, here too the sizes are small. But, you will find high quality designer and name brand clothes and accessories including Courrèges, Paloma Picasso, Sonia Rykiel, among others.

Eighth Arrondissement

DESIGNER JEWELRY
EVE CAZES
20 rue de Miromesnil, 8th arrondissement
Métro Miromesnil
Open Monday to Saturday 11 to 7
Tel: 01 42 65 95 44

Designer jewelry on consignment is what you'll find in this boutique. Mme. Cazes has a degree in gemology from the *Institut National de Gemmologie* which enables her to select the best designer rings, watches, necklaces, bracelets, and so on. You will find names such as Cartier, Boucheron and Van Cleef & Arpels, in vintage and contemporary styles at up to a 50% reduction (bearing in mind that this does not mean low prices!).

GOOD SELECTION
GRIFF-TROC (women)
17 boulevard de Courcelles, 8th arrondissement
Métro Villiers
Open Monday to Saturday 10:30 to 7
Tel: 01 42 25 86 07

You'll find an excellent selection of designer clothes in top condition including suits, and separates. Labels can include Chanel, Yves St Laurent, Kenzo and others. They also have a great collection of accessories such as scarves, belts, purses, jewelry and shoes. At the time I visited, there were no pants.

Ninth Arrondissement

GRANNY'S ATTIC
MAMIE (men, women & children)
73 rue de Rochechouart, 9th arrondissement
Métro Anvers or Barbès
Open Tuesday to Friday 11:15 to 1:30 & 3 to 8, Saturday 2 to 8
Tel: 01 42 82 09 98

Mamie means granny in French and that's exactly the atmosphere you'll find here (or, more specifically, granny's attic). Vintage clothing is crammed into an extremely small and narrow space, so claustrophobics, beware. Be careful when you climb up and down the rickety stairs. Above is a collection of bric-a-brac and below is a heap of shoes that Imelda Marcos would have loved. (Watch your head climbing the stairs!)

Eleventh Arrondissement

SALVATION ARMY EQUIVALENT
EMMAUS (men, women and children)

54 rue de Charonne, 11th arrondissement
Métro Ledru Rollin
Open Monday to Saturday 10:30 to 12:30 & 2 to 6
Tel: 01 48 51 64 51

This is the French equivalent of the Salvation Army for used clothes. Since everything is donated rather than resold, the prices are incomparably low, although the quality is uneven. They also have accessories such as scarves and shoes. If you're in the area it's worth taking a look. Emmaüs is an association created in 1949 to aid socially and economically disadvantaged people in France with job training and loans. It and its founder Abbé Pierre are very well known by the French. Emmaüs Alternatives was founded in 1987 specifically to deal with clothing donations.

Other location:
105 boulevard Davout, 20th arrondissement, Métro Porte de Montreuil, Tel: 01 46 59 13 06

Twelfth Arrondissement

CLEARLY LABELED
MARIE T. (children)
76 boulevard Soult, 12th arrondissement
Métro Porte de Vincennes
Open Tuesday to Saturday 10 to 1 & 3 to 7
Tel: 01 43 42 29 23

This small store is simply packed with used children's clothes in excellent condition. Everything is clearly labeled, and there are shoes, toys, and baby carriages, among other things. The ages range is from 0 to 10 years old.

ARRANGED BY AGE
BAMBINI TROC (children)
26 avenue du Bel Air, 12th arrondissement
Métro/RER Nation
Open Tuesday to Saturday 10 to 1 & 2:30 to 6:30
Tel: 01 43 47 33 76

Another small store, Bambini Troc is also bursting with used children's clothes, in fine condition. The age range, as for Marie-T is roughly from 0 to 10 and everything is carefully arranged by age.

Thirteenth Arrondissement

SPACIOUS AND WELL ORGANIZED
HALF AND HALF (women)
28 avenue des Gobelins, 13th arrondissement
Métro Gobelins
Open Monday 2:30 to 7, Tuesday to Saturday 10 to 2 and 2:30 to 7
Tel: 01 43 36 91 15

The last time I was here, there were wedding gowns in the window. They might have been used, but you'd never know! Inside, the store is spacious with all the clothes clearly arranged by size. They have just about everything and it's all in top condition. The accessories, such as jewelry, are also tops.

Fourteenth Arrondissement

SMALL BUT GOOD CHOICE
TROC PARNASSE (women)
58 rue du Montparnasse, 14th arrondissement
Métro Edgar Quinet

Open Tuesday to Saturday 11:30 to 7:30
Tel: 01 43 22 72 53

Although small, Troc Parnasse has a fine choice of used designer clothes, including names such as Guy Laroche, for reasonable prices. Not only is the quality good, but the owner is very friendly.

TINY BUT GOOD CHOICE
PRISCILLA (women)
4 rue Mouton Duvernet, 14th arrondissement
Métro Mouton Duvernet
Open Tuesday to Saturday 10:30 to 1 & 2 to 7
Tel: 01 45 39 30 03

The shop is tiny yet the selection is good. So, don't go out of your way, but if you're in the neighborhood it's worth taking a look.

SOME LARGE SIZES
TROC MOD (women)
230 avenue du Maine, 14th arrondissement
Métro Alésia
Open Tuesday to Saturday 11 to 7
Tel: 01 45 40 45 93

In this medium sized store there is a section with large sizes. Coats and jackets are also well represented. Prices are reasonable.

Fifteenth Arrondissement

CLASSIC STYLES
L'ASTUCERIE (women and children)
105 rue de Javel, 15th arrondissement

Métro Charles Michel

Open Monday 4 to 7, Tuesday to Friday 12 to 2 & 3 to 7, Saturday noon to 6

Tel: 01 45 57 94 74

The women's styles here tend to be classic rather than youth oriented and they have accessories such as Hermès scarves and Vuitton bags in excellent condition. The children's section is large and includes infant care items as well.

Sixteenth Arrondissement

MUST SEE STORE

LES CAPRICES DE SOPHIE (women)

24 and 28 avenue Mozart, 16th arrondissement

Métro Ranelagh

Open Monday 2 to 6, Tuesday to Saturday 10:30 to 6:45

Tel: 01 45 25 63 02

This is a great store. It is full of used designer clothes of top quality and even a few runway models, worn an hour or two for a fashion show. Certainly, it's in a very upscale neighborhood where many French women have a rather large clothes budget! I especially liked the jackets when I visited. Don't mind the dog if he wants to enter the store—he's part of the family!

DONATED ELEGANT CLOTHES

LES ORPHELINS APPRENTIS D'AUTEUIL (men, women & children)

40 rue de la Fontaine, 2nd store on the left of the courtyard, 16th arrondissement

Métro Jasmin

Open Monday to Friday 2:30 to 6 and the first Saturday of each month (closed in August)
Tel: 01 44 14 76 79

All the clothing in this large space is donated to support a charitable organization, founded in 1866, devoted to helping children in trouble. Since the people donating tend to be wealthy, occasional designer originals can be found for rock bottom prices. Plan to spend a little time here as the selection is huge. You will also find household items such as sets of Limoges china and hand embroidered tablecloths for very low prices.

SMALL BUT GOOD CHOICE
PASSY PUCES (women)
6 rue François Millet, 16th arrondissement
Métro Jasmin
Open Monday 3 to 7, Tuesday to Saturday 11 to 1 & 3 to 7
Tel: 01 45 25 41 36

One of the oldest *dépôt-ventes* in Paris, Passy Puces, though small, has an excellent selection of both accessories and clothes, especially skirts.

ELEGANT STYLES
DEPOT-VENTE DE PASSY (men and women)
14, 16 and 25 rue de la Tour, 16th arrondissement
Métro Passy
Open Monday 2 to 7, Tuesday to Saturday 10 to 7 (Men's store at #25 closed Monday)
Tel: 01 45 20 95 22 and 01 45 27 11 46

The clothing here is very elegant with an excellent selection of Dior, Yves St Laurent, Chanel, etc. in bright colors (this, too, is a store in a wealthy neighborhood). Suits especially are of top quality and choice. The young man who manages the men's store has recently upgraded the choices there.

KIDS CLOTHES & TOYS
SAPERLI & POPETTE (children)
28 boulevard Exelmans, 16th arrondissement
Métro Exelmans
Open Tuesday to Saturday 10:30 to 1:30 & 2 to 7
Tel: 01 45 20 28 02

Another small shopped packed to the brim with clothes, Saperli & Popette also carries kids videos, bikes, toys, shoes, and baby care items such as carriages. The age range is from 0 to 16 years old.

CLEARLY DISPLAYED
FABIENNE (men)
77 bis rue Boileau, 16th arrondissement
Métro Exelmans
Open Tuesday to Saturday 10 to 1:30 & 2 to 7:30
Tel: 01 45 25 64 26

Contrary to most resale shops, Fabienne only sells men's clothes. The styles are varied and are well displayed with sizes clearly labeled. Prices are reasonable for suits, separates and ties.

BIG, BIG, BIG
RECIPROQUE (men & women)
88, 92, 93, 95, 101 & 123 rue de la Pompe, 16th arrondissement
Métro Rue de la Pompe
Open Tuesday to Friday 11 to 7:30, Saturday 10:30 to 7:30
Tel: 01 47 04 30 28

Welcome to the biggest complex of clothing resale stores in Paris. Founded in 1978 by Nicole Morel, it now takes up practically the entire block! Most of the stores are grouped together, except for #123 (women's coats, hats and raincoats) which is down the street a ways, but is worth checking out too. Prices here are definitely high, although less than for new, but the selection and range is unbeatable. In #88 are antiques and gifts; in #92, women's jewelry, scarves, bags and lingerie; in #93, women's evening and cocktail dresses; in #95, women's shoes, daytime and sports clothes; in #101, men's clothes; in #123, women's coats, raincoats (*imperméables*) and hats. Be prepared for a great collection of designer scarves and shawls and a whole rack of Chanel suits (don't worry, the missing buttons have been removed on purpose and will be sewn back on at no extra cost at the time of sale).

Seventeenth Arrondissement

SMALL BUT GOOD
TROC MITAINE (women)
18 rue Pierre-Demours, 17th arrondissement
Métro Ternes
Open Tuesday to Friday 10:30 to 7, Saturday 10:30 to 1 & 3 to 7
Tel: 01 45 74 61 21

The quality and selection here reflect the upper class neighborhood which surrounds this small store. Prices are reasonable considering the quality of the designer labels.

CLEAR LABELS
L'APRES-MIDI (women)
23 rue Brunel, 17th arrondissement
Métro Argentine

Open Monday to Friday 1:30 to 7
Tel: 01 45 74 00 25

You'll have to knock to be let into this tiny shop, but it's worth the effort. The clothes are very clearly labeled with the designer's name on outfits, separates and accessories such as jewelry and bags.

SPACIOUS, ORDERLY & WELL-LIT
DEPOT-VENTE DU 17ᵉ (men & women)
109 rue de Courcelles, 17th arrondissement
Métro Courcelles
Open Monday 2 to 7:30, Tuesday to Saturday 10 to 7:30
Tel: 01 40 53 80 82

The store is orderly and well lit. All the better to take in an excellent selection of designer label clothes in almost perfect condition. Americans in particular will appreciate the spaciousness and clarity of the displays.

UNBEATABLE PRICES
GUERRISOL (men, women & children)
19, 29, 31 and 33 avenue de Clichy, 17th arrondissement
Métro Place de Clichy or La Fourche
Open Monday to Saturday 10 to 7
Tel: 01 42 94 13 21

It isn't glamorous; it doesn't sell designer clothes; it's in a poor work-a-day neighborhood and it's one of the best known stores in Paris for used clothes (used with a capital "U"). There are piles upon piles and racks upon racks of used clothes spread out over several stores. You simply can't beat the price. The secret is that they buy used clothing collected by non-profit associations all over France and Europe. After being washed, ironed and disinfected, the items are then sent to the various stores. So, if you have an eagle eye and are willing to spend some time sifting, bargains (that's with a capital "B") can be found.

Other location:
17 bis boulevard Rochechouart, 9th arrondissement, Métro Barbès-Rochechouart, Tel: 01 42 80 66 18

DEPARTMENT STORES

While I do not generally recommend shopping in Parisian department stores if you want to find a bargain, there is one exception. Twice a year there are big sales: July (with a spillover into August) and January (with a spillover into February). If you come to Paris during these two periods— check out the department stores. As mentioned at the beginning of the new clothing section, these are sales that are regulated by the French government. During other months, the stores can have special promotions, but the official sales periods are the only times they are permitted to put previous store items on sale. So, you can find some things at greatly reduced prices.

As I mentioned in the introduction, in order to get the tax refund (*le détaxe*) you have to spend 1200 FF in one day in one store. If you have a lot of different things to buy, you are definitely better off shopping in a department store where you can get a tax refund of about 13%. However, if you plan to spend that much on one item, such as porcelain or clothing, you might be better off in a smaller store where you will receive the full tax refund of about 16%. You can also ask the individual merchants if they will give you a discount of 10% since you can get this much off at a department store with your discount card (see below). The more you buy, the easier it is to get this discount or even more since the smaller stores know they have to be competitive.

Discount Cards

La Samaritaine, Printemps, Galeries Lafayette and Le Bon Marché provide tourists with 10% discount cards. Check out the lobby of your hotel or the Paris Tourist Office (Office de Tourisme de Paris) at 127 avenue des Champs Elysées, 8th arrondissement, Métro/RER Etoile. Since they are usually out of stock of one or more of the cards, you will probably have to get one or more of them directly from the store. These cards are great, especially since you can usually get an additional 10% off the sales price!

Grouping Purchases

Some of the department stores allow you to purchase in several departments by presenting a coupon instead of money and then pick everything up and pay all at once just before you leave the store. You can also apply for your tax refund at the same time if you qualify.

Here is a list of the major department stores in Paris:

MUST SEE BASEMENT
BAZAR DE L'HOTEL DE VILLE (BHV)
52 rue de Rivoli, 4th arrondissement
Métro Hotel de Ville
Open Monday to Saturday 9:30 to 7 (open Wednesday to 10)
Tel: 01 42 74 90 00

Unfortunately, they don't have a discount card in this store and the staff tends to be not very friendly. So, why go there? Number one reason: the hardware store in the basement (*sous-sol*). It's the largest I have ever seen in my entire life, and you can literally find anything (i.e. hard to find light bulbs, widgets to fix unfixable items, etc.). The prices are not the best, but the selection is, especially if you are a do-it-yourselfer. They also have, on the ground floor (*rez-de-chaussée*), one of the best scarves departments in

Paris plus a good selection of stockings. On other floors you'll find the latest in housewares, fabrics, more do-it-yourself supplies, appliances and lamps, among other things.

CLASSIC STYLE
GALERIES LAFAYETTE
40 boulevard Haussmann, 9th arrondissement
Métro Chaussée d'Antin/La Fayette
Open Monday to Saturday 9:30 to 6:45 (open Thursday to 9)
Tel: 01 42 82 34 56
Web Site: http://www.galerieslafayette.com

This is one of the old standbys, and it's divided into three stores: Galfa Club (for men), LaFayette Sport and the main store. Once inside the main store, have a look at the wonderful glass dome and art nouveau details. Clothing is basically organized by numerous designer concessions.

For your discount card, go to Welcome Desk just inside the rue de Mogador entrance. Be prepared to show your passport and information about your hotel. On the other side of the store, also on the ground floor, is a *caisse* (cash register) where you can pick up a *Carnet d'achats emportés* booklet with the coupons to group your purchases. When you're ready to pay, go to the *Carnets d'achats* office located in the basement. Be aware that you can choose between two consignments, one where you pay and the other at the back of the store on the rue de Provence. The second consignment is open 24 hours a day (this seems impossible, but that's what they say!) and is accessible by car.

You may also be interested in the free fashion show every Wednesday at 11 am. It's an amazing show as incredibly tall thin models prance along the runway in incredibly tall thin clothes. Enjoy the fantasy! Reservations are required at 01 48 74 02 30. The shows take place on the seventh floor of the main store. Use the rue de Mogador entrance and be sure to arrive a bit early to get a good seat since there's usually a crowd.

Other location:
Centre Commercial Montparnasse, 14th arrondissement, Métro Montparnasse

MUST SEE LOOKOUT POINT
LA SAMARITAINE
19 rue de la Monnaie, 1st arrondissement
Métro/RER Pont Neuf, Louvre, Châtelet/Les Halles
Open Monday to Saturday 9:30 to 7 (open Thursday to 10)
Tel: 01 40 41 20 20

The name comes from a statue which was on the top of an old water pumping station built on the Pont Neuf under Henri III. The current building was designed in 1900 to replace the original store nearby founded by Ernest Cognacq in 1869. The large store windows were the first in Paris, inspired by a department store built in Chicago in 1899. You can also see the only remaining grand staircase in a Parisian department store. Although it's not presented very well, and it's hard to get a good view, underneath the dirt the facade is a beautiful and creative blend of art and technology in the art nouveau style.

The store is actually divided into four stores: #1: Toys (one of the biggest selections in Paris), #2: Main store, #3: Sports, and #4: Leisure. You enter the main store where the rue Pont Neuf and the rue de la Monnaie meet the Seine. The basement, which sells hardware items, is almost as good as BHV, but with a much friendlier staff. Also at the top of the main store is a terrace and lookout point where you have a great bird's eye view of the city. The terrace is on the 10th floor and the Lookout (*Panorama*) is on the 11th. I highly recommend the *Panorama* since you end up inside a circle that has all the famous buildings and monuments painted on it, pointing to the actual thing. For your discount card, go to the Customer Service Department (*Service Clientèle*) in the basement of the main store and ask for the *Carte Privilège*. You will have to show your passport.

MOST UPSCALE/GOURMET FOOD STORE
~~LE BON MARCHE~~
22 rue de Sèvres, 7th arrondissement
Métro Sèvres Babylone
Open Monday to Friday 9:30 to 7, Saturday 9:30 to 8
Tel: 01 44 39 80 00

Bon marché means "inexpensive" or "good buy" in French. So, of course, this is the most expensive of the Parisian department stores! Also the world's first department store. It is divided in two, the main store, Store #1 and La Grande Epicerie de Paris, Store #2, (see below), which is open Monday to Saturday 8:30 to 9. Founded by Aristide Boucicaut in 1852, Le Bon Marché made three major innovations: prices were fixed and clearly marked, price mark-ups were low to encourage volume sales and customers were allowed free entry without obligation to buy. (Previously, just entering a store implied that you would purchase something.)

Because it's a little off the beaten track, Le Bon Marché is less touristy than the other department stores and more upscale. Be sure to see the central space in the main store. Filled with light, it's totally elegant, including escalators that dramatically sweep into the open space. Le Bon Marché is also known for it's stylish and creative window displays.

If you want to group your purchases, you can ask for a *Carnet d'Achats* or Shopping Book at the visitor's desk in the main store near the entrance at Rue du Bac. To pay and pick up your purchases, go to the third floor. You also have the choice of having the goods delivered or shipped. The escalator to the third floor is a little hard to find, but it's just behind the Marriage Frères boutique, next to the vacuum cleaners.

La Grande Epicerie de Paris is actually a huge gourmet supermarket. They bake the bread right on the premises and have a nice selection of wine, beautiful arrangements of fruits and vegetables, plus assorted gourmet items. This would be a great place to buy food for a picnic on the Seine river front.

YOUNGER STYLES
PRINTEMPS
64 boulevard Haussmann, 9th arrondissement
Métro Havre Caumartin, RER Auber
Open Monday to Saturday 9:35 to 7 (open Thursday to 9)
Tel: 01 42 82 50 00
Web Site: http://www.printemps.fr

Printemps is also divided into several different stores. You have Printemps de la Mode (fashion), Printemps de la Maison (household) and Brummel (men's fashion). You may be interested to know that Printemps is known for being more in tune with the latest fashion trends than the other department stores.

Pick up your discount card at the Welcome Service on the ground floor of Printemps de la Mode near the entrance opposite Marks and Spencer Store. Be prepared to show your passport. This is also where you can pick up a *Carnet d'Achats* or Purchase Book which you can use to group your purchases. Be aware that as in Galeries Lafayette, there are 2 consignments. One is in the *Espaces Services* in the basement (*sous-sol*) where you pay and the other is on the rue de Provence, at the back of the store. Here too, as in Galeries Lafayette, the separate consignment is open 24 hours a day (!) and is accessible by car.

They also have a terrace on the 9th floor of Printemps de la Maison which is almost as nice as the one at La Samaritaine.

Other location:
Centre Commercial Italie 2, 13th arrondissement, Métro Place d'Italie,
Tel: 01 40 78 17 17

SUPER DISCOUNT
TATI
2 to 42 boulevard Rochechouart, 18th arrondissement
Métro Barbés-Rochechouart
Open Monday to Saturday 9:15 to 7
Tel: 01 42 55 13 09
Web Site: http://www.tati.fr

Besides clothing (see listing in *New Clothing*-18th arrondissement),
Tati has departments for kitchen ware, household items, towels and linen,
dishes, toys and luggage. They say that even rich people come here (under-
cover I guess) because they can't resist the bargains! Nobody knows how
they do it, but the prices are really low. I leave it to your eagle eye to judge
what is quality and what is not.

Other locations:
Aux Deux Marionniers, 38 boulevard Rochechouart, 18th arrondissement, Métro Barbès-Rochechouart, Tel: 01 42 55 13 09 (household only)
    13 place de la République, 3rd arrondissement, Métro République, Tel:
01 48 87 72 81

Tati Or: Tati now sells 18 carat gold jewelry certified by the French
government both in their existing department stores and in new stores
known as Magasins Tati Or (*or* means gold in French). This has not been
good news for the more expensive jewelry stores in the neighborhood!

Other locations (Tati Or)
19 rue de la Paix, 2nd arrondissement, Métro Opéra, Tel: 01 40 07 06 76

132 bd St Germain, 6th arrondissement, Métro Odéon, Tel: 01 56 24 93 15

96 rue St Lazare, 9th arrondissement, Métro St Lazare, Tel: 01 48 74 09 48

113 rue du Faubourg St Antoine, 11th arrondissement, Métro Ledru Rollin, Tel: 01 40 02 03 13

42 avenue du Général Leclerc, 14th arrondissement, Métro Denfert Rochereau, Tel: 01 45 39 83 20

30 rue du Commerce, 15th arrondissement, Métro Emile Zola, Tel: 01 45 78 17 26

75 rue de Passy, 16th arrondissement, Métro Passy or La Muette, Tel: 01 45 27 40 80

FLEA MARKETS

Introduction

The major flea markets (*marchés aux puces*) in Paris are run by licensed dealers. So, although the prices are definitely lower than in antique and second hand stores, they reflect this fact. If you really want to look carefully and seriously (*chiner*) at rummage sales (*brocantes*), you might want to find out where the non-professionals are. There are two excellent French magazines where, even if you don't read French, you can check out the lists at the back. Look for the word *foire* (fair) which means that normal everyday people can sell off their goods without the usual bureaucratic hassles from the French government. Also be on the lookout for *vide-greniers* (attic sales, I guess they have more attics than garages!).

Both magazines can be found at any news stand. One is called *Aladin* which, besides lists of all the *puces* (flea markets) and *foires* in Paris and all over France, has articles with tips on how to look for second hand goods and on collecting. It comes out once a month. The other publication which is really more of a newspaper, comes out every Friday and is called *La vie du collectionneur*. It concentrates on how to collect and the latest "in" things.

Both publications also list special antique/secondhand markets in Paris which take place on an annual basis. And, they let you know about the big antique/secondhand markets and fairs outside of Paris such as the one in early September in Lille, billed as "The Biggest Flea Market in Europe."

For more information, you can visit the web site of the tourist office in Lille: http://www.lille.cci.fr/tourisme/oft106.html.

If you want to venture outside of Paris for smaller *brocantes* and *foires*, (where the best buys and bargains really are), the lists at the back of both magazines are very complete and cover all of France.

While you happily wander around Paris, you may be lucky enough to stumble upon a sign saying *Grande Braderie* posted on the outside of a church. Rejoice! You have just found a church rummage sale, a great place to find real bargains, usually located in the *crypte* (don't worry—that means the church basement!). It's well worth the effort to circle around the church to find the entrance.

There is also a listing of auctions (*ventes aux enchères*) in a weekly events publication called *Pariscope* that is also sold at all news stands. The auctions are hidden at the very end of the "Arts" section. (And at the back is an insert in English that lists special events, exhibitions, films, etc. compiled by the British company Time Out.)

Paris Flea Markets

That said, here are the major flea markets in Paris, or just outside.

First, remember to acknowledge the merchants by saying "Bonjour" when you enter their stands. This will put you off to a good start. Then, speak French if you can. That will continue the good start! Be prepared to pay with cash rather than a check or credit card so you can negotiate a bit (What's your best price? or "Quel est votre meilleur prix?"). Many merchants will lower their prices, at the end, by 20 to 30%, although it helps to know price ranges to begin with. Speaking of cash, keep it carefully hidden as there are usually gangs of pickpockets who circulate around all the flea markets.

If you buy an item over 100 years old, you'll need a certificate of authenticity to avoid customs duty when shipped or carried home. An advantage of authorized dealers is that they can do this. And, they can also help you with shipping, which can be expensive, so be sure to calculate that into the final price. You may also be entitled to a *détaxe* (tax refund) form, so ask for that too.

I have listed opening and closing hours, but frankly, they vary according to the discretion of the merchants! Some arrive earlier than others, stay later, leave earlier, etc. Some of the best deals can be made literally as the dealers unload their trucks in the morning. So, early birds definitely have an advantage (so they say—I'm not one of them).

PUCE DE SAINT-OUEN (Saint-Ouen is just to the north of Paris)
Métro Porte de Clignancourt
Open Saturday between 8 & 9 to 5:30 & 6:30, Sunday 9 & 10 to 5:30 & 6:30 and Monday 9 & 11 to 5 & 6:30 (all very ish).
Friday is open for other dealers.

Finding Your Way There

If you take the metro to Porte de Clignancourt, you then have a 5 to 10 minute walk before you reach the market. Take Avenue de la Porte de Clignancourt and ignore all the junk stands set up on the sidewalk. This is not the market! As a matter of fact, it's much better to walk on the right hand side of the street since all the junk stands are on the left hand side, and it's terribly crowded. The market starts on the far side of the white overpass, on the left.

Rue des Rosiers is the main street with most of the markets. Once you go under the overpass, Rue des Rosiers starts on the left, at an angle. Once you follow rue des Rosiers, turn onto rue Paul Bert (it starts here so you can only turn in the right direction!) which will lead you to rue Jules Vallès. You can also find rue Jules Vallès starting at rue Henri Fabre (the main street that borders the market on the Paris side).

Actually, don't worry about the directions! Just take your time to wander around and enjoy the atmosphere. What I like about this flea market, the biggest in the world, is the sense of being in another place and time, far away from the "real" world. You'll have a sense of being removed from everyday reality, and the more you wander, the better it gets. This may compensate for the fact that you probably won't find super bargains here, although the prices are less than inside Paris proper. You also have all the advantages of buying from authorized dealers (like if any problems come up later, you know where to find them!).

The official market is organized into sub-markets, each with it's own character and atmosphere. City walls used to separate Paris from the outside areas, and many of the poor people who used to live on the "other side" of the wall sold junk and old clothes to survive. Plus, they escaped city taxes! By the 1880's people from Paris were already coming here to buy secondhand items. Around 1920, when the walls were destroyed, the dealers organized themselves into official markets. As you wander along, you'll also see private businesses among the official sub-markets.

Believe it or not, Saint-Ouen is pronounced Sant-Wan (more or less).

Here is a list of the sub-markets:

MARCHE ANTICA
99 rue des Rosiers
This is a new and high class market.

MARCHE BIRON
85 rue des Rosiers
The fanciest, most formal and elegant market, Biron has genuine antiques and a good selection of furniture.

MARCHE CAMBO
75 rue des Rosiers
Although serious and with genuine antiques, Cambo is a little less fancy than Biron. It's a bit hard to find, so look for the entrance opposite Marson Beys, one of the private markets.

MARCHE DAUPHINE
140 rue des Rosiers
This is one of the newest and most modern markets.

MARCHE JULES-VALLES
7-9 rue Jules Vallès
Not as serious as some of the other markets, Jules Vallès has lower prices for good, old-fashioned rummage. It's second best after Paul Bert.

MARCHE LECUYER-VALLES
20 rue Jules Vallès
This is a small, friendly and junky market (you never know).

MARCHE MALASSIS
142 rue des Rosiers
A new market, Malassis is not as interesting as some of the others.

MARCHE MALIK
53 rue Jules Vallès
They used to sell *fripes* (secondhand clothes) here, but Malik is now stuffed with junky new clothes. Spare yourself the effort.

MARCHE PAUL BERT
96 rue des Rosiers and 18 rue Paul Bert
Begun just after World War II, Paul Bert is considered by many to be the best market. Here you can find good deals if you have a good eye. Be sure to visit Madeleine, my friend's cousin who has a stand that sells fire irons, grills and other chimney accessories. It's stand 59, *Allée* (aisle) 1.

MARCHE DES ROSIERS
3 rue Paul Bert

A mere 12 stalls specialize in Art Nouveau (*style 1900*).

MARCHE SERPETTE
110 rue des Rosiers
Serpette is dark, formal, fancy and has genuine antiques.

MARCHE VERNAISON
99 rue des Rosiers
This large and varied market is the oldest.

PUCE DE MONTREUIL
avenue du Professeur André Lemierre, 20th arrondissement
Métro Porte de Montreuil
Open Saturday, Sunday and Monday 8 to 6(ish)

If you have any ideals about how charming, quaint and tasteful Paris is—don't come to this market! I'm afraid that all your illusions will be shattered when you arrive at what has to be the ugliest and junkiest market in France. (It's kind of hard to charming stuffed onto a gigantic asphalt parking lot). The one and only reason to come out here is if you are hunting for bargains in secondhand clothes. They must buy them by the pound (oops, kilo), and if you have an good eye and don't mind sifting, you can find incredible buys. Be prepared to be pushed and jostled since it can get very crowded as the day wears on.

Finding Your Way There
After you exit from the metro, Porte de Montreuil, look around until you see Hotel Ibis in the distance. Then move in that direction towards a traffic circle. Go left around the circle, then to the left into the market. At this entrance are the *fripes* (secondhand clothes).

PUCE DE VANVES
avenue Georges Lafenestre and Marc Sangnier, 14th arrondissement
Métro Porte de Vanves
Open Saturday and Sunday 7 to 2(ish)

This is one of the best flea markets in Paris, relaxed and informal with its combination of licensed and un-licensed dealers sitting behind tables set up on the sidewalk. You can find an enormous selection of bric-a-brac. This is just a partial list of what you can find: buttons, miniature cars, old books, puppets, jewelry, chests of drawers, paintings, military medals, religious statues, birdcages, top hats, plus teddy bears in various states of disrepair. At one part of the market, trees overhang the street, so you can hear birds singing in the background as you stroll along. "Quelle atmosphere!" If you want to maintain your image of quaint and charming Paris, come to this market!

Finding Your Way There
As you exit the metro Porte de Vanves, look for the overpass that crosses Boulevard Brune. Face the overpass and turn left onto Avenue de la Porte de Vanves which will take you to Avenue Marc Sangnier at one end of the market. Follow Avenue Marc Sangnier to the continuation of the market on Avenue Georges Lafenestre. The market is L-shaped.

GIFTS

Gift Suggestions

Here are some suggestions for best buy gifts. First are food gifts, which you can buy in supermarkets and gourmet food stores. Second, body care items which you can find in Parfumeries (listed in Perfumes and Cosmetics) and in Para-Pharmacies, all over Paris. You can also find wonderful soaps, especially *savons de Marseilles* made with vegetable oils and scented with lemon, vanilla, lavender, etc. Or, look for perfumed bath salts and plant-based hair products. There are also tee shirts that you can buy in the souvenir shops listed in the *Souvenirs and Postcards* chapter. Otherwise, you can use the following list.

BEST BUY TIP: Sometimes, when I need to buy a small gift, I go to the Ile St Louis and walk down the main street (rue St Louis en l'Ile, what else?) from the bridge facing Notre Dame towards rue des Deux Ponts. There are numerous gift stores with imaginative gifts ranging from jewelry to unique household items.

First Arrondissement

BODY CARE, PERFUMES & SCENTED CANDLES
L'OCCITANE
1 rue du 29 Juillet, 1st arrondissement
Métro Tuileries

Open Monday to Saturday 10:30 to 1:30 and 2:30 to 7:30, Sunday 12 to 7
Tel: 01 47 03 45 54

This company, based in the south of France, manufactures and sells skincare products, perfumes and scented candles in very attractive packaging. The prices are reasonable.

Other locations:
55 rue St Louis en L'Isle, 4th arrondissement, Métro Cité or Sully Morland
18 Place des Vosges, 4th arrondissement, Métro St Paul
26 rue Vavin, 6th arrondissement, Métro Vavin (located in an old pharmacy with wood paneling and antique bottles on display)
84 avenue Champs Elysées, 8th arrondissement, Métro George V

DESIGNER SCARVES
D'ORLY
242 rue de Rivoli, 1st arrondissement
Métro Concorde
Open every day 10 to 7
Tel: 01 42 60 73 33

Among the many gift stores on the rue de Rivoli, this one has some good prices for designer scarves.

NATURAL MATERIALS
NATURE ET DECOUVERTE
Carrousel du Louvre Shopping Center, 1st arrondissement (To find: get off the Métro at the stop Palais Royal and take the exit Carrousel du Louvre or if you are above ground, face the Louvre, then turn

right and walk along rue de Rivoli until you find the sign which says
"Carrousel du Louvre.")
99 rue de Rivoli,
Métro Palais Royal
Open Monday and Wednesday 10 to 10, Thursday to Sunday 10 to 8
Tel: 01 47 03 47 43

This is a good place to find gifts with a natural bent since everything is
made from non-synthetic materials. Although some of the prices are high,
I especially like the writing paper and envelopes in hand-made textured
paper which are quite reasonable. You can also find jewelry, candles,
incense, toys, bird feeders, plus books and tapes and even refrigerator
magnets. You might also be interested to know that Nature et Decouverte
has a foundation that supports nature preservation and 10% of the store's
profits go into this foundation, one of the largest in France.

BEST BUY TIP: Since the French tend not to send cards, they are
hard to find. You can, however, find outstanding hand-crafted stationary.

Other locations: (all closed on Sunday)
Forum des Halles Shopping Center, rue Pierre Lescot, 1st arrondisse-
ment, Métro/RER Châtelet-Les Halles, Tel: 01 40 28 42 16
Les Trois Quartiers Shopping Center, 23 boulevard de la Madeleine,
1st arrondissement, Métro Madeleine, Tel: 01 49 27 07 58
Italie 2-Grand Ecran Shopping Center, place d'Italie, 13th arrondisse-
ment, Métro Place d'Italie, Tel: 01 45 88 28 28
61 rue de Passy, 16th arrondissement, Métro La Muette, open 10 to 7:30,
Les Quatre Temps Shopping Center, 92 La Défense, Métro/RER La
Défense, Tel: 01 47 75 02 69

BEST BUY TIP: The easiest way to enter the Louvre is through the
Carrousel du Louvre shopping center—less waiting in line!

Museum Stores

Also in the Carrousel du Louvre shopping center are several gift boutiques associated with the Louvre.

You'll find the stores (with the exception of the Boutique Musées et Création) just past the security checkpoint where you enter the Louvre from the shopping center. When in the shopping center, head toward the inverted Pyramid, then, as you face Virgin Megastore, the security checkpoint is to your left. You'll find the Boutique Musées et Création in the corridor to your right, as you face Virgin Megastore (it's called Allée du Carrousel). All these stores are closed on Tuesday since the Louvre is closed on that day.

LOUVRE STORES

In the **Boutique Musées et Création** (open Wednesday to Monday 10 to 8) are porcelain and glass objects created by contemporary artists.

In the **Carterie du Musée du Louvre** (open Wednesday and Monday 9:30 to 9:30 and Thursday, Friday, Saturday and Sunday 9:30 to 7) are reproductions of paintings from the Louvre and other museums in postcard and poster formats. The store has two parts. On one side of the corridor are the postcards and on the other, posters.

In **Monnaie de Paris** (open Wednesday 9:30 to 9:30 and Monday, Thursday, Friday, Saturday and Sunday 9:30 to 8) you can find coin reproductions produced by the Musée de la Monnaie, jewelry, reproductions of sculptures, golden medallions and earrings.

The **Librairie (bookstore) du Musée du Louvre** (open Wednesday to Monday 9:30 to 9:30) has a large selection of items including art books, calendars, engravings, jewelry, all the way to tee shirts and scarves. There is also a room of books for kids (all in French, of course), including coloring books on the upper floor.

The **Chalcographie** (open Monday and Wednesday 9:30 to 9:30 and Thursday, Friday, Saturday and Sunday 9:30 to 7) sells maps and engravings.

NON-LOUVRE STORES

You'll find the children's store **Le Ciel est à Tout le Monde** in the Allée du Carrousel (to the right of Virgin Megastore). Items to look for are cute postcards and small items such as modeling clay and children's books. For anyone who is a "Little Prince" nut, there are several "Little Prince" items, the best buy being a coloring book (*Le Petit Prince Album à Colorer*).

In **Le Comptoirs du Patrimoine**, also on the Allée du Carrousel, the only best buy items are creative post cards.

Another store on the Allée du Carrousel is **Flammarion 4** where you can sometimes find end of series artistic tee shirts and posters.

MUSIC BOXES (NOT DISCOUNT BUT GO ANYWAY)
ANNA JOLIET
9 rue de Beaujolais, 1st arrondissement
Métro Palais Royal
Open Monday to Saturday 10 to 7
Tel: 01 42 96 55 13

Anna Joliet sells music boxes in all shapes, forms and sizes. You'll find music boxes shaped like a miniature grand piano or a bird in a cage, made of wood, see through, and even attached to a key chain. You can also take a stroll into the courtyard of the Palais Royal, which takes you back to another time and place when life was less hectic. It's a very special place where you can tranquilly window-shop, eat or admire the garden in the center.

HOUSEHOLD ITEMS
POTIRON
57 rue des Petits Champs, 1st arrondissement
Métro Pyramides
Open Monday to Saturday 10 to 8
Tel: 01 40 15 00 38

In this small but pleasant store you will find all sorts of clever household item gifts including sets of porcelain and silverware in primary colors and plastic bottle stoppers.

TEA ACCESSORIES
COMPAGNIE ANGLAISE DES THES
Shopping Center Forum des Halles, Niveau (level) -3, 3 rue Basse, 1st arrondissement
Métro/RER Les Halles
Open Monday to Saturday 10 to 7:30
Tel: 01 40 39 95 43

This store sells wonderful teapots. Plus tin tea containers and a selections of exotic teas, mugs and tea sold in bulk.

SECOND ARRONDISSEMENT

CREATIVE & IMAGINATIVE TOYS
SI TU VEUX
68 Galerie Vivienne, 2nd arrondissement
Métro Palais Royal

Open Monday to Saturday 10:30 to 7
Tel: 01 42 60 59 97

The motto of the store is "Les enfants d'abord!" (Children first!) which is an accurate description of what this store is all about. They not only sell delightful and creative toys and games, but they also organize workshops every Wednesday and Saturday on different themes such as creating Halloween masks, Christmas decorations, balloon sculptures, etc. They have over 60 toys and/or games that are exclusive to their stores. Overall they look for quality items at very reasonable prices. There is also a catalog available for mail orders.

Fourth Arrondissement

MUSEUM STORE
PARIS MUSEES
29 bis rue des Francs Bourgeois, 4th arrondissement
Métro St Paul
Open Tuesday to Sunday 11 to 7
Tel: 01 42 74 13 02

Near the Musée Carnavalet is this magnificent museum store where they sell collections of contemporary artists inspired by French cultural history. You can find everything from address books, jewelry, purses, scarves and designer jewelry. For the children they have cutout models of Notre Dame and other subjects. In the museum itself, at 23 rue de Sévigné is the museum store where you can other gift items.

DIFFERENT
ALEXIS LAHELLEK
41 rue des Francs Bourgeois, 4th arrondissement
Métro St Paul

Open every day 10:30 to 7:30
Tel: 01 44 61 72 75

The first thing you'll notice are the bright colors, then the fact that everything is made of inflatable plastic (i.e. inflatable soap dishes, lamps, flower vases, etc.) Easy to pack in the suitcase, right?

JEWELRY
MONIC
5 rue des Francs Bourgeois, 4th arrondissement
Métro St Paul
Open Monday to Saturday 10 to 7, Sunday 2:30 to 7
Tel: 01 42 72 39 15

The selection of quality costume jewelry is great and the prices are reasonable. They also sell designer pieces at reduced prices and can do in-house creations plus jewelry repair.

Other location:
14 rue de l'Ancienne Comédie, 6th arrondissement, Métro Odéon, Tel: 01 48 87 79 19. Closed Sunday.

STATIONARY
PAPIER +
9 rue du Pont Louis Philippe, 4th arrondissement
Métro St Paul or Pont Marie
Open Monday to Saturday noon to 7
Tel: 01 42 77 70 49

As I mentioned earlier, the French love hand-crafted stationary. In this store you will find it in all colors, grades and textures. They also sell beautiful wooden pencil and paper clip holders plus colored pencils.

JEWELRY
SICOMOR BIJOU EUGIT AMOR
20 rue du Pont Louis Philippe, 4th arrondissement
Métro St Paul or Hotel de Ville
Open Monday to Saturday 10:30 to 7:30
Tel: 01 42 76 02 37

This is the place for you if you are partial to wild and crazy designer jewelry. The prices are medium rather than really low.

Other location:
11 rue des Francs Bourgeois, open Monday to Saturday 11 to 7, Tel: 01 42 74 52 37

HAND MADE SOAPS
ZADIG ET VOLTAIRE
12 rue Sainte Croix de la Bretonnerie, 4th arrondissement
Métro Hôtel de Ville
Open Monday to Saturday 11 to 7

If you want to find something truly different, you'll want to check out this store. They sell hand made soaps in all shapes, sizes, colors and smells. In addition, you'll find bath salts and masques and herbs. All the bath products are made from a base of fruits and vegetables, and you can even buy in bulk. This is definitely a "hip" store in a "hip" neighborhood.

PERSONALIZED TEE SHIRT
MAGIC COMPANY
5 bis, rue de la Tacherie, 4th arrondissement
Métro Hôtel de Ville
Open Monday to Saturday 10 to 2 and 3 to 7
Tel: 01 42 74 63 75

If you want a personalized gift, you can have it created for you here. Basically, they print impressions from any flat picture or photo onto any object. For example, you could buy a reproduction of a work of art from the Louvre and bring it to this shop where they will print it onto a tee shirt for a very reasonable price in 1 to 3 days. You bring the drawing, photo or picture, they supply the tee shirt. The only drawback is that they do not speak English (French and Russian yes, English no).

Fifth Arrondissement

FOR CAT LOVERS
LA GALERIE DU CHAT
58 rue Henri Barbusse, 5th arrondissement
RER Port Royal
Open Tuesday to Saturday 10:30 to 7:00
Tel: 01 43 25 31 71

Cat lovers, this is your store! There is a large selection of gifts and every single one has something to with cats (with a few mice thrown in). You'll find mugs, jewelry, postcards, coat hangers, dishes, figurines, stuffed animals. The prices are reasonable.

Sixth Arrondissement

CANDLES
CIR
22 rue St Sulpice, 6th arrondissement
Métro St Sulpice
Open Monday to Saturday 10 to 7
Tel: 01 43 26 46 50

If you like candles, look no further. They have candles in all colors, sizes and formats such as candles shaped like flowers in real flower pots, animals, frogs on lily pads, and lady bugs. They've got floating candles, mosquito repelling candles, religious candles, and so on.

HANDICRAFTS
VILLAGE TIBETAIN
2 rue de Cicé, 6th arrondissement
Métro Notre Dame des Champs
Open Monday to Saturday 10:30 to 7
Tel: 01 45 48 27 88

I happen to like Tibetan handicrafts, especially the woven pouches. They make great gifts and they don't break! The gifts in this out-of-the-way store include jewelry, hand woven and embroidered bags and sacks, multi-colored backpacks, handmade writing paper, and Buddhist ritual objects. You can also find traditional clothing including wool tops and silk tunics.

Seventh Arrondissement

NOT DISCOUNT BUT GO ANYWAY
DEYROLLE
46 Rue du Bac, 7th arrondissement
Métro Rue du Bac
Open Monday to Saturday 10 to 1 and 2 to 6:45
Tel: 01 42 22 30 07

When you step inside this store, you feel as you've gone back in time at least 100 years. Just walk up the magic stairs. Founded in 1831, this taxidermy shop seems more like a mini natural history museum than a store. Imagine stuffed lions, tigers and bears, oh my (the brown bear is hidden inside a side office). If you collect insects and butterflies, you will be in butterfly heaven as you will find all the equipment you need to collect butterflies, plus minerals of France and old maps. This is one of those special stores.

WE SELL EVERYTHING STORE
PLAISIRS
10 Rue du Bac, 7th arrondissement
Métro Rue du Bac
Open Monday to Friday 11 to 7:30, Saturday 1 to 7:30
Tel: 01 40 15 04 54

This is what I call a "we sell everything" store", officially, a *bazar*. They're all over Paris, and they actually do sell a little bit of everything from hardware items, dishes, electrical supplies and cooking utensils to stuffed animals (sometimes at a very good price) and more. This is one of those stores, but in a better neighborhood, so the quality of the goods is better. You will find clothes, household items, travel alarm clocks, flower vases and other assorted gifts.

Eighth Arrondissement

STONES & CRYSTALS/JEWELRY
MINERALES DO BRASIL
86 rue de Miromesnil (2nd courtyard), 8th arrondissement
Métro Villiers
Open Monday to Saturday 10 to 6
Tel: 01 45 63 18 66

You can tell that this is a special store as you pass through mysterious looking arches into the second courtyard at the back. In the small retail outlet to the right there are piles of crystals and semi-precious stones jumbled all about plus polished stone eggs, small boxes, fossils and bead necklaces in stone, hematite, coral and lapis lazuli. This importer of precious stones and crystals supplies retail stores all over France, so the prices here are about 30% less. If you are lucky, they will allow you to see the amethyst room which is in the far corner and is not generally open to the public (When you ask, this is your chance to practice being very formal and polite).

Ninth Arrondissement

TOYS
PAIN D'EPICES
23 Passage Jouffroy, 9th arrondissement
Métro Grands Boulevards
Open Monday 12:30 to 7, Tuesday to Saturday 10 to 7
Tel: 01 47 70 08 68

This delightful store is located in a *passage* or covered shopping gallery of Paris. As you enter the gallery, filled with light coming in through the glass ceiling, you can imagine how things were in the 18th and 19th century which is when the galleries were built. The store itself has old-fashioned toys including hand puppets, small plastic animals (very inexpensive), wooden trains and puzzles and accessories for doll houses, among other things. Be sure to visit the upstairs.

IMAGINATIVE GIFTS
LE COMPTOIR DES PAPILLONS
5 rue Papillon, 9th arrondissement
Métro Poissonnière or Cadet
Open Monday to Friday 11 to 7, Saturday 3 to 7
Tel: 01 42 46 58 10

When you enter this store, you enter into a charming personal space created by the owner, Nathalie Doumie, and you will be pleasantly surprised by this imaginative, upscale gift store in an otherwise dull, business neighborhood. She sells creative gifts here from Greek olive oil and Alsatian jam to hand embroidered linens (by Nathalie herself), perfumed candles, dishes, door stops and other assorted items for the home. There is also a small section with children's toys and stuffed animals. It's all highly eclectic and original

Tenth Arrondissement

HOUSEHOLD ITEMS
LA TISANIERE
21 rue de Paradis, 10th arrondissement
Métro Poissonnière or Cadet
Open Monday to Saturday 10 to 6:30
Tel: 01 47 70 22 80

You can find all sorts of small household gifts here in addition to larger porcelain and earthenware items. In fact, the store is a factory outlet for a porcelain factory northeast of Bordeaux which you can visit and which can personalize designs for you. Information on this and the tours can be found in the store. They also sell their own line of porcelain with patterns based on classic designs.

Eleventh Arrondissement

TRADITIONAL CHILDREN'S TOYS
GAMIN D'VOLTAIRE
149 boulevard Voltaire, 11th arrondissement
Métro Charonne
Open Tuesday to Friday 10 to 6:30, Saturday 10 to 1:30 and 2:30 to 6:30
Tel: 01 40 09 85 00

An abundance of traditional toys are packed into a small space in this store where you'll find a great selection of stuffed animals, a set of miniature snare drums, plus other small toys, all at very reasonable prices. The young man who owns the shop is extremely friendly, and the store is an expression of his personal tastes. This is the sort of store you won't find in the tourist areas.

ODD-BALL
OLGA L'OBJET
261 boulevard Voltaire, 11th arrondissement
Métro/RER Nation
Open Monday to Saturday noon to 7:30
Tel: 01 40 24 00 20

All the gifts in this store are hand selected by the owner. You will find designer baby bottles, wooden ballpoint pens, picture frames, jewelry and lots of oddball objects.

Twelfth Arrondissement

CUTE HOUSEHOLD ITEMS
IDEM
92 rue du Faubourg Saint-Antoine, 12th arrondissement
Métro Ledru Rollin
Open Monday to Saturday 10 to 7
Tel: 01 43 46 39 18

You can find all sorts of small porcelain household items, baskets, picture frames and other small gifts in this store. The prices are very reasonable.

Other location:
88 boulevard des Batignolles, 17th arrondissement, Métro Villiers,
Tel: 01 45 22 20 13

Fourteenth Arrondissement

OUTSTANDING HANDCRAFTED
LA BOUTIQUE DE L'ARTISANAT MONASTIQUE
68 bis avenue Denfert Rochereau, 14th arrondissement
RER Port Royal
Open Monday to Friday noon to 6:30, Saturday 2 to 7 (closed in August)
Tel: 01 43 35 15 76

Here you have an abundance of hand-crafted articles, all made by
monks and nuns in monasteries all over France. The range is quite diverse
including children's clothing and dolls, bedding (hand embroidered),
leather goods, scarves, candles, perfumes, skin products and food such as
candy and honey. You can also find handmade lace. It looks small at the
entrance, but this store includes a large basement where you can wander
around in a sort of tranquil daze, admiring all the handiwork. The sales
staff is extremely friendly, though does not, as a rule, speak English.

Sixteenth Arrondissement

HOUSEHOLD ITEMS
CASA
50 rue de Passy, 16th arrondissement
Métro Passy or La Muette
Open Monday 12:30 to 7, Tuesday to Saturday 10 to 7
Tel: 01 46 47 99 02

This is the place for household items at a reasonable price. The store
looks as small as a postage stamp on the ground floor, but once you go

down into the basement, you realize how big it is. There is also a small upper floor. They have a lot of interesting items on all three levels including candles, teapots, baskets, storage containers, dishes, vases, table linen, plus stuffed animals, picture frames, some furniture and more.

Other location:
92 rue St Lazare, 9th arrondissement, Métro St Lazare, Tel: 01 49 70 01 90

UPSCALE WE SELL EVERYTHING STORE
L'ENTREPOT
50 rue de Passy, 16th arrondissement
Métro Passy or La Muette
Open Monday to Thursday 10:30 to 7, Friday and Saturday 10 to 7
Tel: 01 45 25 64 17

Entrepôt means warehouse and that's just about what you'll find here in another "we sell everything" store or *bazar* in an upscale neighborhood where the quality is better than usual for this type of merchandise. They really do sell just about anything including household items, clothes, and toys. You name it, they've got it.

Eighteenth Arrondissement

ODDBALL
PYLONES
7 rue Tardieu, 18th arrondissement
Métro Anvers
Open Monday 2 to 7, Tuesday to Friday 10:30 to 7 and Saturday 10 to 7:30
Tel: 01 46 06 37 00

Here you will find originally created oddball gifts such as designer cork screws, latex flower vases, rubber towel hooks, etc.

Other locations:
Les 3 Quartiers Shopping Center, Espace Créateurs, 1st floor, 17 boulevard de la Madeleine, 1st arrondissement, Tel: 01 42 61 08 26
52 Galerie Vivienne, 2nd arrondissement, Tel: 01 42 61 51 60
57 rue St Louis en l'Ile, 4th arrondissement, Tel: 01 46 34 05 02

HAND PAINTED SILK SCARVES
NINA CANAL
20 rue Muller, 18th arrondissement
Métro Chateau Rouge
Open Wednesday to Sunday 3:30 to 7 (it's best to phone ahead)
Tel: 01 42 62 08 28

Artisan Nina Canal was born in South Africa and now makes her home in Paris. In this small boutique she displays her hand painted silk, wool and cashmere scarves with original designs inspired by a combination of plant forms and geometric shapes. Each is one of a kind.

PERFUMES AND COSMETICS

Introduction

You have a choice between shops that cater to tourists or those that cater to the French. The tourist shops know all about the *détaxe* or tax refund, but they tend to be small and have all the perfumes stored behind the counter. Since I'm generally a "self-service" shopper, I prefer the French stores where all the perfumes are lined up on the counter, usually in alphabetical order by brand, and I can sample at my leisure without having to ask for help. I have included both kinds of shops, but with a preference for those catering to the French. I believe you get a better sense of what it's like in Paris if you shop where the people who live here shop!

Testing Perfumes

Take advantage of the thin white strips of paper you will find on the counter. I suppose this is obvious, but it took me several years to realize that this allows you to sample a large number of scents without spraying perfume on your elbows (after using up both wrists, arms, backs of hands etc. and becoming totally confused as to what scent you've put on there in the first place). You can also carry the strips around to see how the scent develops with time, which, of course, is very important with the finer perfumes. After you have sprayed perfume on your wrists, do not rub them together to aid the drying process! You can even wave your arms around wildly in the air, but no rubbing allowed. I don't know exactly why, but this rule was forcefully repeated to me by several French friends who know their perfume.

BEST BUY TIP: For the lower end brands, be aware that the French brand Bourjois is owned by Chanel and that the inexpensive brand Gemey is owned by L'Oreal. I really like the Bourjois eyeshadows.

FREE SAMPLES: Many stores give out free samples, but sometimes you have to ask for an *échantillon gratuit.*

First Arrondissement

GUERLAIN AT A DISCOUNT
MARIONNAUD PARFUMERIES
120 rue Rambuteau, 1st arrondissement
Métro Les Halles
Open Monday to Saturday 10 to 7
Tel: 01 40 26 49 00
Web Site: http://www.marionnaud.com

This French chain is acquiring new stores all the time, so they're just about everywhere and far too numerous to list. All the major brands of perfumes and cosmetics are available, most at a discount of up to 25%, and they do the *détaxe* or tax refund forms. The stores in the suburbs outside Paris sell Guerlain at a discount (which they can't do inside Paris because of the Guerlain stores). The store in Levallois is large and covers two floors. If you plan to shop here regularly, remember to ask for your *carte de fidelité.*

Other locations outside Paris (open 9:30 to 7:30):
19 rue d'Alsace, 92 Levallois-Perret, Métro Louise Michel, Tel: 01 47 37 98 98

56 and 110 avenue Charles de Gaulle, 92 Neuilly-sur-Seine, Métro Les Sablons, Tel (#110): 01 47 45 25 02

123 rue de Paris, Les Lilas, Métro Mairie des Lilas, Tel: 01 43 63 73 41

146 rue de Fontenay, 94 Vincennes, Métro Chateau de Vincennes (open Tuesday to Saturday, 9 to 7:30 and Monday afternoons), Tel: 01 43 98 18 18

DETAXE SPECIALIST
CATHERINE
6 rue de Castiglione, 1st arrondissement
Métro Concorde or Tuileries
Open Monday 10:30 to 7, Tuesday to Saturday 9:30 to 7
Tel: 01 42 61 02 89

This small boutique is the champion of the détaxe specialists. Although small, all major name brands are available and you can be assured of receiving the correct tax refund. Even if you don't qualify, prices are discounted up to 25% depending on the brand.

Second Arrondissement

CATERS TO TOURISTS
MICHEL SWISS
16 rue de la Paix, 2nd floor (UK), 3rd floor (US), 2nd arrondissement
Métro Opéra
Open Monday to Saturday 10 to 7
Tel: 01 42 61 61 11

You won't find this *parfumerie* showing its display window on the street, because it's several flights up in an elegant building on rue de la Paix. Find the number and then take the elevator or stairs up to the store. There you will find a large array of cosmetics in all the major brands,

French and otherwise, (Dior, Armani, Chanel, Gaultier, Lancôme, Yves St. Laurent, etc.), discounted up to 35%. In the back you'll find men's ties, scarves, pens, leather goods and costume jewelry. Most of the sales staff speaks English (among other languages).

Other location:
24 avenue de l'Opéra, 1st arrondissement, Métro Pyramides, Tel: 01 47 03 49 11

Third Arrondissement

TYPICALLY FRENCH
RAYON D'OR
178 rue du Temple, 3rd arrondissement
Métro République
Open Monday 10:30 to 7, Tuesday to Saturday 10 to 7
Tel: 01 42 72 03 76
Web Site: http://aurayondor.fr

Almost all the major brands of cosmetics and perfumes are sold at up to 30% off, and there's a different promotion each week.

Other locations:
94 rue St Lazare, 9th arrondissement, Métro St Lazare, Tel: 01 48 74 30 38
13 rue du Faubourg Montmartre, 9th arrondissement, Métro Grands Boulevards, Tel: 01 45 23 13 86

Eighth Arrondissement

MUST SEE STORE!
SEPHORA
70 avenue des Champs Elysées, 8th arrondissement

Métro George V
Open Monday to Saturday 10 to midnight, and Sundays noon to midnight
Tel: 01 53 93 22 50

Just down the street from Planet Hollywood, Sephora really deserves a visit simply because it's one of the most beautiful stores you'll ever see. As you enter the grand entrance, you march down a ramp into the store. The decor is very high tech, and the store itself is huge. Second, on either side, you'll see bottles and bottles of perfumes arranged in alphabetical order by brand (my kind of store!). Each type has a tester (plus the little white strips of paper, naturally). Go for the experience even if you don't buy anything.

There are other locations, but this store is so much more impressive, that I haven't listed the others!

Ninth Arrondissement

THEATRICAL MAKEUP
MAKI
9 rue Mansart, 9th arrondissement
Métro Blanche
Open Tuesday to Saturday 11 to 1 and 2:30 to 6:30
Tel: 01 42 81 33 76

I like theatrical makeup. It's long lasting, the colors are great, and—it's cheap! This store is located in the heart of one of Paris's theater districts where it sells to actors, models and makeup artists.

MUST SEE
PARFUMERIE FRAGONARD
9 rue Scribe, 9th arrondissement
Métro Opéra

Open Monday to Saturday 9 to 6, Sunday 9:30 to 4:30
Tel: 01 47 42 04 56

First, take advantage of the free perfume exhibit upstairs, with descriptions in English, displayed in an elegant former mansion. On the ground floor you'll find an outlet store for Fragonard, a perfume maker located in Grasse (the perfume center of France) which has been in existence for almost 300 years. What you might not know is that they manufacture several scents of very high quality that are extremely close to designer originals, but for a lesser price, of course. L'eau Fantasque is close to L'eau de Kenzo; Concerto is similar to CK One, and Emilie is almost the same as Paris by Yves St. Laurent. There are other scents as well, including a Shalimar smell-alike called Rêve Indien plus perfumed soaps, skincare products and scented candles. All the sales staff speaks English.

Tenth Arrondissement

UNIQUE
PLANTADERM
58 rue du Faubourg Poissonnière, 10th arrondissement
Métro Poissonnière
Open Monday to Saturday noon to 6:30 (closed in August)
Tel: 01 42 46 42 88

This special store is hidden away in a courtyard, so look for the sign on the front gate of the building. Basically, it's a factory outlet store where the skin and hair care products are all made from natural ingredients, either vegetable or marine.

The owner used to be a pharmacist who noticed that most of the beauty products sold in his pharmacy contained only a small amount of formula and lots of filler. Thinking he could do as well or better, he took some cosmetology courses and in 1983 literally mixed his first batches of products in his kitchen sink! They sold so well in the pharmacy, that he quit to devote himself full time to developing hair, nail and skincare formulas which he then sells to designer brands.

I love the lotions, creams, *sérums* and shampoos while I'm not as happy with the makeup except for lipstick no. 30 which appears to be too pink but is, in fact, a fantastic lip gloss. Monday to Friday a beautician (*esthéticien*) is on hand to help you choose the right products and to give facials. And, here too you'll find perfumes similar to but not exactly like designer scents. No. 801 is like Ombre Rose; no. 802 is like Trésor; no. 803 is like Montana; no. 804 is like Ysatis; no. 805 is like Shalimar and no. 806 is like Anaïs (more or less).

Sixteenth Arrondissement

SPECIAL STORE
PARFUMS DE NICOLAI
69 avenue Raymond Poincaré, 16th arrondissement
Métro Victor Hugo
Open Tuesday to Friday 10 to 6:30, Saturday and Monday 10 to 1 and 1:30 to 6:30
Tel: 01 47 55 90 44

Filled with blue and golden yellow light, this store invites you in to find distinctive perfumes created by Patricia de Nicolaï, the grand daughter of Guerlain (there's a perfume laboratory in the back room). Although most of the staff does not speak much English, the service is friendly and—you can always point! I sampled *L'eau d'été* (summer water) and it was a light, citrusy scent that lasted a long time. They sell everything from toilet water to perfume, scented candles, collector bottles and room scents, and the prices are reasonable. This is one of those special stores where even if you don't buy a thing, it's still worth the trip.

Other locations:
80 rue de Grenelle, 7th arrondissement, Métro Rue du Bac, opens at
1:30 on Tuesday, Tel: 01 45 44 59 59

All Over Paris

FRUIT SCENTED PERFUMES
YVES ROCHER

This skin care and makeup chain is all over Paris. It deserves a mention
for its fruit scented eau de toilettes. My favorites are *Pomme* (apple) and
Pêche (peach) which are light and refreshing in summer. I also like *Vanille
Bourbon* (I think you can guess what this means!). If you plan to shop here
regularly, be sure to ask for a *carte de fidelité* which really does add up to
free gifts and price reductions.

PRODUCE MARKETS

Introduction

One of the greatest things about Paris, as we all know, is the food. One of the reasons it's so great is the quality of the raw ingredients. In every neighborhood of Paris there are weekly produce markets where you can find an astounding array of fresh fruits and vegetables, cheese, poultry, meat, fish plus non-food items such as household goods, clothes, dishes and so on. Following is a list of a few of my favorite markets, both indoor and outdoor. If you're in the mood for a picnic and/or you just want to sample some of the best fresh food you've ever had, you've definitely got to visit a local market. You can get a complete list of all the markets (in French) at the *Hôtel de Ville de Paris* or Paris Town Hall, just opposite the department store BHV on the rue de Rivoli. Just ask for it at the reception desk.

BEST BUY TIP #1: Some of the best bread can now be found at stands in the produce markets. The new trend is toward bread baked in wood-burning ovens, using natural yeast and a blend of flours.

BEST BUY TIP #2: If you're really at a loss as to which stand to go to, just look at the lines of people waiting and go to the stand with the longest line. French people generally know their food and are demanding shoppers—go where they go!

Outdoor Markets

All the markets listed have the same hours: 9 to 1

Maubert Market
5th arrondissement
Place Maubert, Métro Maubert
Tuesday, Thursday, Saturday
This is a good market for food specialties and crafts from the provinces. As in most markets, there are also jewelry and other odds and ends besides food. This is a small, but high-quality market.

Monge Market
5th arrondissement
Place Monge, Métro Place Monge
Wednesday, Friday, Sunday
There's a lot packed into this space. Besides the usual assortment of fresh produce, you can find wine, CD's, honey, clothes and tablecloths. In a word, this market is small but good.

Raspail Market
6th arrondissement
boulevard Raspail between rue du Cherche Midi and rue de Rennes, Métro Rennes or Sèvres Babylone
Tuesday, Friday, Sunday (organic) (Rennes is closed on Sunday)
The Sunday organic market is small but varied. You can find fresh herbs, natural fiber clothes, costume jewelry, silk blouses, incense, natural soap besides the usual assortment of produce, cheese, pasta, bread and more. There's also a stand with homemade jam (with free samples). The weekday market has a good selection of everything including wool skirts, foie gras, tablecloths, girls' dresses and women's blouses.

Saxe Breteuil Market
7th arrondissement
avenue de Saxe, from avenue de Ségur to the place Breteuil, Métro Ségur
Thursday, Saturday
Within sight of the Eiffel Tower, this pleasant market has an excellent selection of food items, plus assorted clothing, lace, wine, purses, fresh pasta and porcelain dishes. You can even find Albanian pizza (!).

Batignolles Market (organic)
8th arrondissement & 17th arrondissement
boulevard des Batignolles on the center divider strip between no. 27 & 35 (8th) and no. 34 & 48 (17th), Métro Place de Clichy/Rome
Saturday
This delightful market specializes in natural and organic (*biologique*) foods, both fresh produce and take-out dishes. With all the food crises lately, this is becoming more and more popular in France. You can also find raw silk blouses, mare's milk, wine and sushi, all in the same space! This is a great market to visit to pick up a picnic lunch.

Bastille Market
11th arrondissement
boulevard Richard Lenoir, from rue Amelot to rue St Sabin, Métro Bastille
Thursday, Sunday
This large and busy market has so many stands that it's a little hard to make a choice. As a matter of fact, it's the largest in the city.

Popincourt Market
11th arrondissement
boulevard Richard Lenoir, between rue Oberkampf and rue de Crussol, Métro Oberkampf
Tuesday, Friday

Another large (no, let's call that huge) market with a large variety of stands (including sewing machines). There's even a stuffed boar at one of the cold cut stands.

Auguste Blanqui Market
13th arrondissement
boulevard Auguste Blanqui odd no. side between Place d'Italie and rue Baurrault, Métro Place d'Italie
Tuesday, Friday, Sunday
This market snakes along the street in a long, thin path and has a good range of products and produce.

Edgar Quinet Market
14th arrondissement
center divider strip of boulevard Edgar Quinet, Métro Edgar Quinet
Wednesday, Saturday
Here you have an excellent selection of produce and products including leather goods, watches and watch repair and wine.

Grenelle Market
15th arrondissement
boulevard de Grenelle, between rue Lourmel and rue du Commerce, Métro La Motte Picquet-Grenelle
Wednesday, Sunday
This market takes place under the elevated tracks of the Paris Métro. Besides the usual selection you can find clothes, bedding, tablecloths, fresh ground coffee and tea, and socks.

St Charles Market
15th arrondissement
rue St Charles between rue de Javel and the Rond Point St Charles, Métro Charles Michels

Tuesday, Friday

I believe that this is one of the best markets in Paris. You not only have the market stands, but you also have the stores facing them. The selection is great including bakeries, CD's, leather goods, jewelry, caned chairs (plus restoration), and even mattresses and box springs. Many of the stores sell gourmet takeout food…and all this in sight of the Eiffel Tower!

Président Wilson Market

16th arrondissement

center divider strip of avenue du Président Wilson between rue Debrousse and Place d'Iéna, Métro Alma Marceau/Iéna

Wednesday, Saturday

This is a lovely market with great inexpensive clothes for kids besides a good selection of produce and products.

Barbès Market

18th arrondissement

side road of boulevard de la Chapelle facing Hôpital Lariboisière, Métro Barbès

Wednesday, Saturday

You can pretend that you have taken a side trip to North Africa here. Be forewarned that you may have to push your way through the crowd. This market is animated, inexpensive and you can find great olives!

Ordener Market

18th arrondissement

rue Ordener between rue Montcalm and rue Championnet, Métro Jules Joffrin

Wednesday, Saturday

As in all the higher quality markets, here you can find fresh pasta and wine besides fantastic produce.

Dejean Market

18th arrondissement

rue Dejean, Métro Château Rouge

Tuesday to Sunday 10 to 1 & 3 to 7 (approximately)

Here you can pretend you're in Central Africa. It's a little dingy, but what the heck—you've got atmosphere! Besides the produce, there are fresh fish stores that sell exotic fish not found elsewhere in Paris. It's crowded with Africans, some in traditional dress, doing their shopping.

Indoor Covered Markets

St Germain Market

6th arrondissement

48 rue Lobineau, Métro Mabillon or Odéon

Tuesday to Friday 8 to 1 & 4 to 8, Saturday 8 to 1:30 & 4 to 8, Sunday 8 to 1:30

Set to one side of an elegant shopping center, Marché St Germain displays a small but elegant selection of fresh produce, cheese, meats and other fresh ingredients, plus gourmet take-out. You'll also find wine and fresh bread.

Aligre Market

12th arrondissement

Place d'Aligre, Métro Ledru Rollin

Tuesday to Saturday 8 to 1 & 4 to 7:30, Sunday 8 to 1

On your way to the covered market are the fruit and vegetable stands, piled high with fresh produce. It's loud, lively and can get pretty crowded on the weekends. As you continue toward the Place d'Aligre, watch out for the shopping carts! Eventually you'll find the covered market with specialty stands for cheese, fish, meat, poultry, coffee & tea, flowers and Italian food.

Passy Market

16th arrondissement

at the corner of rue Bois le Vent and rue Duban, Métro La Muette

Tuesday to Saturday 8 to 1, Sunday 8 to 1

This is a small market in the middle of an up-scale shopping street, rue de Passy. The ceilings are high, giving it a light and airy feel. At one end you can choose from live fish swimming in a tank. At the other stands a stuffed fox overlooking the mushrooms.

Batignolles Market

17th arrondissement

96 bis rue Lemercier, Métro Brochant

Tuesday to Saturday 8 to 12:30 & 4 to 7:30, Sunday, 8-12:30

Hidden in a more remote neighborhood, this large and busy covered market is impressive. Besides the stands in the market, there are food specialty stores on the street rue des Moines, which runs along the market. It's definitely worth checking out if you're in this neighborhood.

Ternes Market

17th arrondissement

8 bis rue Lebon, Métro Ternes

Tuesday to Saturday 8 to 1 & 4 to 7:30, Sunday, 8 to 1

There is a nice selection of food here including fresh ground coffee, pastries, olives, all in a harmonious, relaxed atmosphere. Plus, the streets leading up to the market (rue Lebon and rue Bayen) are pretty good too.

La Chapelle Market

18th arrondissement

10 rue de l'Olive, Métro Marx Dormoy

Tuesday to Saturday 8-1 & 4-7:30, Sunday, 9 to 1:30

I had to list this market since this is where I do my weekly shopping! Although the market is small, the merchants are great. You can find terrific fresh vegetables and fruits, fresh fish, poultry and meat and there are 2 great cheese stands besides stands for olives and dried fruit. It's not large enough to warrant a special trip, but come on by if you're in the neighborhood (which, though not pretty is lively and *sympa,* or nice!).

Shopping Streets

There are also shopping streets all over the city filled with food and other specialty stores. You can usually find terrific fish, cheese, baked goods, take-out food, cold cuts, etc. The hours are approximately 9 to 1 and 4 to 7:30 Tuesday to Saturday and 9 to 1 on Sunday. Here's a partial list:

Rue Mouffetard from rue de Bazeilles to Place de la Contrescarpe, Métro Censier Daubenton or Place Monge
The produce stands are at the bottom of the hill. As you walk up, you'll find restaurants and gift stores.

Rue de Buci and rue de Seine, Métro Odéon
This street has a little of everything, even a Champion supermarket. It's in one of the oldest sections of Paris and looks just like what you'd imagined Paris to be.

Rue Cler, from rue de Grenelle to avenue de La Motte Picquet, Métro Latour Maubourg
Lively and with the added charm of cobblestones, this street displays a great variety of fresh and prepared food, including health food. Also check out rue St Dominique which has several great bakeries (just follow your nose!) and an assortment of other small shops.

Rue de Lévis, Métro Villiers
This is a charming pedestrian shopping street. You've got a good selection of food, leather goods and clothing stores. The food stores include

baked goods, cold cuts and cheese. If you're lucky, you might even run into a street musician playing away.

Rue Bayen where it meets rue Poncelet, Métro Ternes

Some of the best takeout food in the city can be found on these two shopping streets. You will find top cheese stores (including Alléosse Roger, one of the best cheese shops in Paris), roast chicken, and fish stores (including Daguerre Marée, one of the best fish stores). There are also fresh vegetables and fruits, a coffee roaster, several bakeries, a wine store, etc. Yet another food shopping area overflowing with goodies.

Rue des Abbesses, Métro des Abbesses (as you exit the Métro, face the church and turn right)

This picturesque shopping street is at the foot of Montmartre and has the same charm as the rest of the area.

Rue Duhesme between rue du Poteau and rue Ordener, Métro Jules Joffrin

In only one block they really pack in the food. There are a lot of small stores which open out onto the street. It is small but lively. You can also check out rue du Poteau and rue Ordener which have many small specialty shops and bakeries.

Souvenirs and Postcards

In the tourist areas of Paris you will find both inexpensive Paris souvenirs (key chains, pins, coasters, T-shirts, paper weights, refrigerator magnets, and so on) plus postcards. These areas include:

The rue de Rivoli from the Palais Royal to Concorde
I found the best prices for Paris T-shirts at Melisa, 170 rue de Rivoli, Métro Palais Royal, Tel: 01 42 96 48 73 (it's one of the first stores as you start walking from Palais Royal).

The quai St Michel and quai de Montebello between boulevard St Michel and Notre Dame Cathedral
At # 11 quai St Michel you'll find a good selection of T-shirts, including Sorbonne T-shirts and sweatshirts. The owner is Indian and so speaks excellent English. # 9 quai St Michel also has a good selection.

The boulevard St Michel, in front of the Musée Cluny
The stands here are good for *Université* T-shirts and sweat shirts.

The rue d'Arcole and the rue du Cloître Notre Dame just behind Notre Dame Cathedral
Esmeralda at 1 quai aux Fleurs, Métro Cité, Tel: 01 43 29 54 93, is one of the best Paris souvenir shops behind Notre Dame Cathedral. Their prices are very reasonable. Another good shop is Paris Notre Dame, at the

intersection of rue du Cloître Notre Dame and rue Chanoinesse. Here you'll find Napoleon bottle openers and Paris erasers.

The rue de Steinkerque near the Place St Pierre at Montmartre, following along the Place to the rue Tardieu
Some of the tee-shirt prices are too high here, so check in several stores before you buy.

Boulevard Haussmann between Métros Havre-Caumartin and Chausée d'Antin
You'll find T-shirts and other souvenirs in the stands outside the department stores Galeries Lafayette and Printemps

Special Postcards

First Arrondissement

LIBRAIRIE PAPETERIE BEL-GAZOU
Passage des 2 Pavillons at 5 rue des Petits Champs, 1st arrondissement
Métro Pyramides
Open Monday to Saturday 7:30 to 7:30
Tel: 01 42 61 21 00

This small shop is tucked away in a small *passage* or gallery, and you will find a good selection of art cards.

LES DRAPEAUX DE FRANCE
34 Galerie Montpensier in the Palais Royal, 1st arrondissement
Métro Palais Royal
Open Tuesday to Saturday 11 to 6
Tel: 01 40 20 00 11

This is another small shop with an excellent selection of art cards including Colette and old shots of Paris.

MEMO ART
Shopping Center Galerie du Carrousel du Louvre, 1st arrondissement
Métro Palais Royal
Open Monday 11 to 8, Tuesday 11 to 7, Wednesday 10 to 10, Thursday to Sunday 10 to 8
Tel: 01 42 86 54 70

The postcards are great. Otherwise, this is a very expensive store.

ARTISTES SANS FRONTIERES
Shopping Center Forum des Halles, Niveau (Level) -3, 13 Grand Galerie, 1st arrondissement
Métro Les Halles/RER Châtelet Les Halles
Open every day 10 to 8
Tel: 01 45 08 53 88

The postcards in this store are artistic and unusual.

Other location:
62 rue St Denis, 1st arrondissement, Métro Les Halles/RER Châtelet Les Halles

Fourth Arrondissement

POMPIDOU CENTER
4th arrondissement
Métro Rambuteau
Just opposite the Pompidou Center (Tel: 01 42 71 60 50) is **Magasin Soho**, 113 rue St Martin, open 10 to 9, where you'll find a large selection

of postcards at reasonable prices. Just around the corner at 9 rue St Martin is the store **MONA LISAIT** where you will also find good prices. (Tel: 01 42 74 03 02.) **LA FONTANA**, 12 rue Brisemiche, (Tel: 01 42 77 64 28) which also has a large selection of postcards and prints is opposite the fountain, to one side of the Pompidou Center. They also sell elaborate bookmarks. All three stores are open every day.

SORBONNE
4th arrondissement
Métro St Michel or Cluny-La Sorbonne/RER St Michel or Luxembourg
Near the Sorbonne at 41 boulevard St Michel is **LE GRILLON**, a stationary store with an excellent selection of special postcards at low prices. It's open 9:30 to 7 Monday to Saturday, (Tel: 01 43 54 28 24). Just down the street, facing 47 boulevard St Michel is a news stand that, believe it or not, has as good a selection of cards as most stores, and at low prices.

Eighteenth Arrondissement
HALLES ST PIERRE
2 rue Ronsard, 18th arrondissement
Métro Anvers
Open every day 10 to 6
Tel: 01 42 58 72 89

The cards are to be found in the bookshop attached to this small arts center. The selection is outstanding, plus there is usually an interesting exhibit to visit. I have actually bought cards here that were so beautiful that I couldn't bear sending them out!

AU PIED DE LA LETTRE
5 rue Tardieu, 18th arrondissement
Métro Anvers

Open Monday to Saturday 10:30 to 6
Tel: 01 46 06 14 05

This small stationary and bookstore carries beautiful artistic postcards at a reasonable price and the couple that owns the store is
extremely friendly.

SUPERMARKETS AND HYPERMARKETS

Introduction

The best known and most widely available supermarket chains in Paris are Monoprix and Prisunic which are basically variety stores with a food section upstairs, downstairs, or in the back of the store. The house brand at Monoprix's variety store is *Miss Helen* which is usually less expensive than competing brands. For products such as chocolates, herb teas (*infusions*), etc., the house brand is *Monoprix Gourmet*. Some other chains in Paris are: Casino, Atac, Leader Price and Champion. You'll also see a lot of Franprix's, which are smaller versions of your basic supermarket. Ed l'Epicier (called by its letters "uh-day") is a discount supermarket, so discount, in fact, that they do not even supply bags. It's bring your own or buy one at the check out. Don't expect to find the same brands each time you go back, since they buy large quantities of close-out items.

At most markets, if you buy produce, you have to weigh it yourself on scales in the produce department. You may be surprised to find that the frozen food section is usually rather small and uninteresting. This is because there are stores that specialize in frozen foods. The best known chain is Picard.

Here are a few special supermarkets that are worth noting:

LARGE CHOICE
INNO, 31 rue du Départ, 14th arrondissement
Métro Montparnasse
Open Monday to Saturday 9 to 9
Tel: 01 45 78 73 06

First, the variety store part is really great. They've got a good selection of clothes, toys, cheap make up, socks, umbrellas, etc. Downstairs in the food department, which is enormous, you can find all kinds of gourmet items including takeout, wines and alcohol, and a stand of Hédiard, a well known gourmet food brand. The selection is better than in most ordinary supermarkets, and you can also find an excellent selection of household items.

LIKE IT SAYS IN THE NAME—GOURMET
LAFAYETTE GOURMET, 48 boulevard Haussmann, 9th arrondissement
Métro Chausée d'Antin
Open Monday to Wednesday and Friday to Saturday 9 to 8, open Thursday 9 to 9. Also open the first 3 Sundays in December.
Tel: 01 49 95 08 71

On the second level of the Monoprix next to Galeries Lafayette is the supermarket with the best selection of gourmet food outside the special gourmet shops such as Fauchon. They've got a great selection of chocolate and candy, wine and alcohol, cheese, pasta, preserves and more. Plus, they have a lot of take-out gourmet food—I even found some bagels at the bakery stand just outside the checkout. It's a mix of the normal and the sublime. This is a great place to buy food gifts to bring back home as it has a vast array of typically French food, and yet it's cheaper than many of the specialty stores. The easiest way to enter is to go straight back into the Monoprix and then take the escalator up.

OLD STANDBY
LA GRANDE EPICERIE, 38 rue de Sèvres, 7th arrondissement
Métro Sèvres-Babylone

This is a huge, wonderful gourmet supermarket which is part of Le Bon Marché department store. (See Department Stores.)

CHINESE
TANG FRERES, 48 avenue d'Ivry, 13th arrondissement
Métro Porte d'Ivry
Open Tuesday to Friday 9 to 7:30, Saturday and Sunday 8:30 to 7:30

This is *the* Chinese supermarket of Paris, right in the middle of Chinatown. It looks like a warehouse at first, but keep going and you'll see the entrance. Just outside are takeout stands. Inside you'll find a large selection of Chinese and Asian food products plus fresh produce including some exotic fruits and vegetables you've probably never seen before. Note: There's another Tang Frères just down the street but it's smaller and not as interesting.

Hypermarkets

Hypermarkets are huge warehouse size stores that sell food and everything else from automobile tires, bikes, stereos, vacuum cleaners, clothes, computers, videos and more. Since they buy in large quantities, the prices are the lowest anywhere. You will not find any hypermarkets (or *grandes surfaces* which means literally "large space") inside Paris because it's simply too expensive to rent or own so much space. You can, however, find some just outside the borders of the city. I don't think it's worth making a special trip, but if you happen to be in the area, why not check it out? This is where the majority of French people outside Paris do the majority of their shopping. I guess it's the flip side of small, intimate Paris shops.

Since hypermarkets are designed to serve people with cars, they are not usually near public transportation. So, be prepared to walk a bit if you don't have a car.

Auchan, in Centre Commercial (shopping center) Les Quatre Temps, La Défense, Métro/RER Grande Arche de La Défense, Tel: 01 41 02 30 30

Note: If you take the Métro, the stop is two zones. However, if you take the RER train, it's three zones which means the ticket is more expensive. And remember to keep your RER ticket because you'll need it to exit from the station.

Auchan, 26 avenue du Général de Gaulle, Bagnolet, Métro Porte de Bagnolet, Tel: 01 49 72 62 00

Carrefour, 1 avenue du Général Sarrail, 16th arrondissement Métro Porte d'Auteuil, Tel: 01 40 71 33 00

Centre Leclerc, 55 rue Deguingand, Levallois-Perret, Métro Louis Michel, Tel: 01 41 27 91 60

Intermarché, 183 avenue Pierre Brossolette, Montrouge, Métro Porte d'Orléans, Tel: 01 46 57 24 29

WINE

BEST BUY TIP: In the chain store called **NICOLAS**, Web Site: http://www.nicolas.tm.fr, they have a house brand of wine called *Petits Recoltes* or small harvests. The prices are extremely low and the quality very good. These are not "great" wines, but are an excellent value for the price, and Nicolas is all over Paris.

In the fall, many of the hypermarkets have a *foire au vin* or wine fair. With their buying power, they are able to offer a large selection of great wine at prices about equal to those at the winery. If you live on the outskirts of Paris, you may receive a mailing. Otherwise, you'll have to contact the *grande surface* nearest to you.

Another choice in Paris for a an excellent selection at fair prices is the supermarket Lafayette Gourmet, 48 boulevard Haussmann, Métro Chausée d'Antin (see listing in *Supermarkets/Hypermarkets*).

So many neighborhoods have great wine stores that it's impossible to list them all. So, here is a short list of Parisian wine stores or *caves* just to give you an idea of what's available.

Second Arrondissement

LARGE RANGE
LEGRAND FILLES & FILS
1 rue de la Banque, 2nd arrondissement
Métro Bourse

Open Tuesday to Friday 9 to 7:30, Saturday 8:30 to 1 & 3 to 7
Tel: 01 42 60 07 12

Founded in 1819 by Lucien Legrand, this store has been in the same location since 1880 and is currently managed by Francine, the third generation of the founding family. The store is known in Paris for having among the best choices for the best prices. They also sell coffee, tea, chocolate, candy, snacks and dried mushrooms besides wine storage accessories.

Fourth Arrondissement

ACCESSORIES
LESCENE-DURA
63 rue de la Verrerie, 4th arrondissement
Métro Hôtel de Ville
Open Tuesday to Saturday 10 to 7
Tel: 01 42 72 08 74

This old-fashioned store is chock full of wine storage accessories including cork screws, decanters, barometers, thermometers and even Swiss army knives.

Fifth Arrondissement

FRIENDLY & GOOD SELECTION
CAVE DU PANTHEON
174 rue St Jacques, 5th arrondissement
RER Luxembourg
Open Tuesday to Saturday 9:30 to 1:30 and 3:30 to 8
Tel: 01 46 33 90 35

The people in this store are very friendly and stacked along the walls you'll find a good selection of wines.

A LITTLE OF EVERYTHING
SARL NECTAR FRANCE
25 rue des Ecoles, 5th arrondissement
Métro Maubert Mutalité
Open Monday to Saturday 10 to 8
Tel: 01 43 26 99 43

In this small neighborhood store near the Sorbonne, they sell a little of everything including "little wines" at low prices, exotic fruit juices and beer.

Sixth Arrondissement

AMERICAN OWNER/WINE TASTINGS
LA DERNIERE GOUTTE
6 rue de Bourbon Le Château, 6th arrondissement
Métro Odéon, St Germain des Prés or Mabillon
Open Monday 4 to 9, Tuesday to Saturday 9:30 to 1:30 & 4 to 9,
Sunday 10:30 to 1:30 & 3 to 7
Tel: 01 43 29 11 62

It's worth making the effort to find this small wine store, especially if you're really serious about wines. The owner is a young American, Juan Sanchez, who originally came to France to be a chef and instead got into the wine business. He's been in this location for several years and would certainly enjoy talking to you about wine. On Saturdays he has wine tastings of estate bottled wine from 11 to 1:30 and 4 to 7:30 with the winemakers present (except during August when the tastings will be by theme).

Eighth Arrondissement

ONE OF THE BEST
CAVES AUGE
116 boulevard Haussmann, 8th arrondissement

Métro St Augustin
Open Tuesday to Saturday 9 to 7:30, Monday 1 to 7:30
Tel: 01 45 22 16 97

Caves Auge is one of the best wine stores in Paris with a good selection of better wines.

SERIOUS
CAVES TAILLEVENT
199 rue du Faubourg St Honoré, 8th arrondissement
Métro Ternes
Open Tuesday to Friday 9 to 8, Monday 2 to 8, Saturday 9 to 7:30
Tel: 01 45 61 14 09

This is a serious place. You can tell by the crowd of French businessmen in suits and ties, besides the fact that it's attached to the famous restaurant of the same name. The wine cellar just below (climate and humidity controlled, of course) contains 600,000 bottles of wine! The selection ranges from mid-range to the stratospheric which you would expect. When ordering, you select from a catalog and the wine is brought to you. Thank goodness the staff is friendly and helpful!

Thirteenth Arrondissement
WELL ARRANGED
LA CAVE DES GOBELINS
56 avenue des Gobelins, 13th arrondissement
Métro Place d'Italie
Open Tuesday to Saturday 9 to 1 & 3 to 8
Tel: 01 43 31 66 79

You will find the wines well organized and labeled along the wall. The price range is from medium to high, with a good selection of different wines.

Fourteenth Arrondissement

GOOD QUALITY/WINE TASTINGS
LA CAVE
197 avenue du Maine, 14th arrondissement
Métro Alésia
Open Tuesday to Friday 10 to 1 & 4 to 8, Saturday 10 to 1 & 3 to 8, Sunday 10 to 1
Tel: 01 45 40 58 18

The street isn't pretty, but the shop is. In it, you will find very good quality at competitive prices. They also have wine tastings (*dégustations*) every Saturday, except during July and August. The schedule is posted on the door. They also sell wine storage accessories and big jars of honey.

Eighteenth Arrondissement

WINE WAREHOUSE
CENTRE DES VINS DE PROPRIETES
Entrepôt Ney Calberson,
Pedestrian entrance: 13 boulevard Ney, 1st floor, 18th arrondissement
Métro Porte de la Chapelle (you have to press the metal button to enter, then take the elevator to N (*niveau*) 1 (level 1)
Car entrance: 215 rue d'Aubervilliers, at boulevard Ney, 18th arrondissement, free parking
Open Monday to Saturday 10 to 7, Sunday 10 to 12:30 (closed Sunday in August)
Tel: 01 40 37 61 50

This is the real thing—a giant warehouse for wine located in the industrial outskirts of Paris where you buy by the case (3, 6 or 12 bottles). So, if you have a car, take advantage of the super selection. This is the biggest wine store in France. They also sell foies gras and pre-cooked regional specialties.

Author photograph by Iris Hart

ABOUT THE AUTHOR

Jeanne Feldman, American, began her career in the film industry in Los Angeles. In 1991 she moved to Paris where she developed her interest in inter cultural relations and best buy shopping. Jeanne joined Inter Cultural Management Associates a management consultant firm, in June of 1999 where she now works on various multi cultural projects.

INDEX

Printed in the United States
23444LVS00005B/346-351